Financing and Managing Projects, Volume I

Financing and Managing Projects, Volume I

A Guide for Executives and Professionals

Prof. Nand L. Dhameja
Prof. Ashok Panjwani
Prof. Vijay Aggarwal

BEP BUSINESS EXPERT PRESS

Financing and Managing Projects, Volume I: A Guide for Executives and Professionals
Copyright © Business Expert Press, LLC, 2017.

First published in 2017 by
Business Expert Press, LLC
222 East 46th Street, New York, NY 10017
www.businessexpertpress.com

ISBN-13: 978-1-60649-668-8 (paperback)
ISBN-13: 978-1-60649-669-5 (e-book)

Business Expert Press Portfolio and Project Management Collection

Collection ISSN: 2156-8189 (print)
Collection ISSN: 2156-8200 (electronic)

Cover and interior design by S4Carlisle Publishing Services
Private Ltd., Chennai, India

First edition: 2017

10 9 8 7 6 5 4 3 2 1

Printed in the United States of America.

Abstract

Project is an instrument of change and no project is complete unless its objective is achieved. Every project is specific and unique. The term project is expanding and ever changing; executives, regulatory bodies and other stakeholders have to look into the managerial and financing aspects of a project.

This Volume deals with the managerial aspects of a project, i.e., project phases, its formulation and appraisal techniques; there is no one best technique and executive judgment is essential.

Every chapter begins with the objectives to be delivered and at the end includes some project instances, brief case examples and case studies so as to provide an analytical kit for executives and professionals

The book makes for a lucid reading and works as a guide for the reader. It has been written based on our experience(s) gained and also the feedback collected from teaching, training and delivering various consultancy projects. Suggestions/comments and feedback are welcome.

Keywords

Discounted Cash flows, Infrastructure and Social Projects, Project Risk, Project Appraisal, Project Definition, Project Life Cycle, Project Monitoring, Public Private Partnership—PPP, Social cost-benefit Analysis, Special Purpose Vehicle—SPV, Time and Cost Overruns, Viability Gap Funding—VGF

Contents

Preface

A project is an instrument of change, and no project is truly successful unless its objective(s) are achieved. Every project has its specific objective(s) and is unique. The term project is evolving and constantly changing; with more and more social and infrastructure projects, the need to have a better understanding of managerial and financing aspects of projects by the executives, regulatory bodies, and other stakeholders, has become central to the successful delivery of projects.

The present book spread over two volumes covers aspects relating to management and financing of projects. Volume 1 deals with the managerial concepts used in a project, that is, project phases, its formulation, and appraisal techniques; of course, there is no one best technique, and executive judgment is very often called upon. The present Volume 2 is devoted to the financing aspects, related in particular, to the infrastructure projects, including the PPP approaches, and project monitoring and the performance measurement through time and cost over-run of projects.

Every chapter begins with the listing of the objectives to be achieved and includes, at the end, certain project instances, brief case examples, and case studies to provide substantive insights into specific areas of project management and financing for executives and professionals.

The book is simple to understand and a comprehensive guide for executives and professionals. The book has been developed on the basis of our experience gained and also feedback received while teaching, training, and consultancy we have provided on various projects. We would welcome suggestions/comments and any feedback on the various aspects of project covered in various chapters, these would be duly acknowledged and be helpful in bringing out the next edition of the book.

We would acknowledge the guidance and encouragement provided by Padmashri Prof Pritam Singh in completing this book. Prof Sanjay Shrivastva, MD and VC, Manav Rachna University, suggested many practical and relevant changes in the presentation of the book, and we would like to convey our heartfelt thanks to him. We are indebted to our esteemed colleagues and well-wishers for their useful and thought-provoking inputs at various stages of development of this book. We are thankful to Business Expert Press for their co-operation and smooth release of the book.

Nand L. Dhameja
Ashok Panjwani
Vijay Aggarwal

CHAPTER 1

Project Management

An Overview

After having gone through this chapter, you should be able to
- Oversee project examples
- Understand the meaning of a project and its distinct characteristics
- Appreciate project significance
- Understand project categorization
- Identify stakeholders of a project and their interest therein
- Oversee project instances, examples, and project management practice

Key Terms: Project, Program, Task, Work Package, Project Significance, Mutually Exclusive Project, Independent Project, Contingent Project, Agencies Interested

Projects: Examples

We come across projects which range in size, cost, time frame, and dimension—local, domestic and international. Some examples are

- Planning for higher education for your son
- Setting up of educational institution—a school or a college

- Replacement of machinery by an industrial house
- Oil refinery construction
- Paltana power project in Tripura in India
- Construction of bridge across river
- Launching of a new product—an advertising and marketing project
- Adoption of six villages in Tripura by ONGC Ltd
- Construction of a charitable hospital by R K Mission
- Wind farm in the middle of ocean
- Construction of Eiffel Tower in Paris
- Construction of Suez Canal
- Arctic Highway: between Tibbit and Contway in Canada
- Setting up of a dairy unit for Rs. 140 crores in Thane district of Maharashtra by milk giant Amul in India
- Acquisition of 100 percent stake in Houghton International Corp. Inc. by Gulf Oil Corporation Ltd, HindujaGroup Co. for $1.04 billion to have larger geographical reach and access to new technologies used in production of highly technical and customized chemical formulation

Project: Meaning

What do we mean by a project and how does it differ from the similar terms program, task, an activity, or work package?

A project is defined as an activity or set of activities which

- is *specific and unique*
- seeks to achieve defined *objectives* with given resources in a *given time*
- involves investment which creates *assets* whose benefits will be *available over time*
- has a cycle: a definite *beginning and an end*
- is an *instrument of change*
- involves allocation of *resources—scarce ones*
- has capital cost, annual cost, and annual benefits

One change always leaves the way open for the establishment of others

Niccolo Machiavelli

Distinct features of a project as indicated above in italics include: it is specific and unique; it serves some objectives and requires resources, output or assets it creates, costs involved, time frame, and stakeholders interested. Project Management Institute's (PMI) Project Management Body of Knowledge (PMBOK) has defined a project as "a temporary endeavor undertaken to create a unique product, service or result."[1] On the other hand, jobs or activities which are of routine nature are non-projects, though such distinction between a project and a non-project gets blurred in many cases.

The term *"project"* is similar to terms *"program," "task,"* and *"work package"*; program is a broader term; it refers to an exceptionally large or voluminous work which encompasses a set of projects. Projects are further divided into tasks or activities which can be combined or put together into work packages. In other words, the terms program, projects, tasks, and work packages indicate the hierarchy of a job in view and have the features of a project. For example, development of a new engine and development of suspension system are parts of the program to develop a new automobile. Similarly, literacy program would involve setting of education institutes, construction of buildings, acquisition of furniture, preparation of books, and training of teachers. Further, urban development program would entail construction of roads or houses or development of civic facilities like water and sewerage system.

Project Management

Project management refers to the collective steps to make the project happen, that is, to take the project to final end to achieve the desired objective. PMBOK defines project management as "the application

---

[1]Project Management Institute, *A Guide to Project Management Body of Knowledge*, 5th ed. 2013.

of knowledge, skill, tools and techniques to project activities in order to meet stakeholder's needs and expectations from a project." Project management is similar to an investment decision or a capital budgeting exercise; it involves investment in long-term assets with the expectation of benefits in coming years. The investment has long-term implications and is a decision-making process to evaluate a proposal to set up a project, or for expansion, or acquisition or replacement of fixed assets, or amalgamation or merger decisions.

A project manager is responsible for the success of the project and is expected to have knowledge of different functions of management, namely, technical, sales and marketing, human resources, production management, and so on. As such, there is an overlap between project management, production management, and technical management. However, project management is multi-disciplinary, normally unique, and non-repetitive, while production management and technical management are not multi-disciplinary and often are repetitive.

Every project has two sides, namely,

- To forecast its expected return
- To evaluate and determine rate of return for the project

Every project involves finances as *outflows* and *inflows*. *Outflows* may be Capital Cost or Operating Costs. Capital cost is one time cost and usually nonrecurring, while operating costs are operation and maintenance costs, relate to normal business operations, and are recurring in nature. Similarly, inflows are nonrecurring or recurring. Nonrecurring inflows relate to raising of fund from the owners or shareholders or from financial institutions or banks for setting-up of the project, while operating revenue refers to stream of sales revenues and is recurring.

A project as such is of concern to

- a state or a state agency, or
- a business enterprise, or
- a family, or
- an individual

Project Significance

Various stakeholders have interest in a project and every project has significance as

- Project investment decisions are linked with objectives, that is, a project focuses on a service generation to increase GDP; or to reduce poverty, or to increase literacy; or to improve profitability or to reduce costs for a business enterprise. For example, under National Rural Employment Guarantee Act (NREGA), every household in rural India has a right to at least 100 days of guaranteed employment every year. Further, National Rural Employment Program (NREP), under the Sixth Five Year Plan, had the objective to alleviate rural poverty by endowing the poor with productive assets or skills so that they can employ themselves usefully to earn greater income and thus cross poverty line.

No project is complete unless its objective is achieved

The Alchemist, Paulo Coelho

- Project Investment proposals are large in number and involve huge amount of investment.
- Project has long life and long-term commitment.
- No going back: Project once selected, any change or modification will be costly or may have catastrophic effects.

There is no going back. And when you can't go back you have to worry only about the best way of moving forward

Paulo Coelho

- Project Investment decision involves
  - exchange of current funds for future benefits, or
  - funds investment in long-term assets, or
  - benefits that will occur over the years.

Project Categorization: Bases

As mentioned earlier, projects have different dimensions in terms of costs, concept, locations, longevity, and purposes they serve. As such, projects can be categorized under three heads on the basis of

- Purposes they serve: economic or social; or
- Segments of the economy; or
- Nature, whether mutually exclusive or independent

These categories many a time overlap and are illustrated below. Projects categorized on the basis of **purpose** they serve include

- Projects having *growth opportunities* like
  ○ Expansion
  ○ Diversification
  ○ Technology upgradation
  ○ R&D
- Projects providing cost reduction opportunities by change of production process or

Cutting costs without improvements in quality is futile

W. Edwards Deming

- Projects having noneconomic justifiable opportunities like
  ○ Pollution Control or Fire Fighting

First two are economically justifiable while the last one is socioeconomic project.

Projects categorized on the basis of **segments** of an economy include

- Industrial projects
- Agriculture projects
- Core sector covering crude oil, petroleum, refinery products, coal, electricity, cement, finished steel
- Infrastructure projects
- Urban infrastructure
- Social projects

Project categorized on the basis of their **nature** include

- *Mutually exclusive projects* where choosing of one rules out the other projects. Projects are mutually exclusive due to size, or timing, or technology.

Some examples are

  ○ acceptance of a project now or later; or
  ○ plan to set up 400 kV power transmission line or 2 × 200 kV lines; or
  ○ plan to set up hydroelectric project at location X or at location Y; or
  ○ choosing between two machines of different sizes or of different technology; or deciding whether to replace an existing machine; or
  ○ whether to manufacture or buy a product.
- *Independent projects* where acceptance or rejection of a project does not eliminate the other projects. For example, acceptance of one or all projects like a sophisticated communication system, or air-conditioning of office premises, or replacement of machinery depend upon availability of funds. It is a situation of capital rationing.
- *Contingent projects* where acceptance of a project depends upon the adoption of one or more other projects. Example, provision of a parking place is contingent upon the construction of the main building.

What agencies/parties are interested in a project?

Project management exercise will depend, to a large extent, on the party or an agency for whom the exercise is being done. Such agencies include

- Promoters, collaborators
- Banks, financiers, development banks
- Vendors
- Government
- Regulatory authorities

First three are primarily interested in commercial aspects of a project, while the last two are also interested in social aspects like regional development or employment generation or pollution control.

As such, for the former, the exercise is called *Commercial* appraisal, that is, to examine the profitability of the project, and is primarily involved with analysis of the financial aspects, while the latter is termed as *Economic* appraisal, which also considers nonfinancial aspects, like social benefits and costs, besides the financial ones. The appraisal principles and process for both are the same and are discussed later.

Instances for Discussion

First Geothermal Plant in Chhattisgarh

A Geothermal Power Plant at Tattapani area of Balrampur district was to be installed by the NTPC and the Chhattisgarh government had granted permission for the same. It would be the first geothermal power plant in the country.

Geothermal generation refers to harnessing of the geothermal energy or the vast reservoir of heat stored in the earth's inner core.

IGI Airport to Get New ATC Tower

Delhi's Indira Gandhi International (IGI) Airport planned to have one of the world's tallest air traffic control (ATC) tower. The proposed tower is nearly double the size of the existing ATC tower. The areas of concern on account of the new tower include space requirement for facilities like training center, recreation facilities, rest areas, and offices.

Cairn India Plans to Revive Oil Hunt

Cairn India, controlled by billionaire Anil Agarwal, plans to start drilling its first new well in 5 years to raise output and help bolster the best profit margin for an oil company in Asia. The company got the Indian government's approval in mid February 2013 to explore new oil pools in its biggest field in Rajasthan and is accelerating its plans to drill 30 wells in the year starting April 1, 2013, and a similar number in the following 12 months.

Reliance–Sibur Plant Construction

Reliance Sibur Elastomers, a joint venture (JV) of Reliance Industries Ltd (RIL) and Sibur started construction of a butyl rubber plant in Jamnagar. The plant was planned to be commissioned in 2015 and would be India's only manufacturer of butyl rubber and the JV will be among the world's top-five manufacturers of butyl rubber. RIL and Russia's Sibur signed the JV in February 2013 to produce 100,000 tonnes of butyl rubber per annum.

New York Co. Plans to Sell Boston Globe

The New York Company plans to sell the *Boston Globe* and other New England properties with an objective to focus its energy and resources on its flagship newspaper. *The Globe* and *The Telegram & Gazette* are described as "outstanding."

InterContinental Plans 47 New Hotels in India

Global hospitality major InterContinental Hotels Group (IHG) planned to open 47 new hotels in India by 2017 there by increasing room strength by 9,882 rooms to over 12,000 in the country.

IHG currently operated 13 hotels in 9 cities across India, including Bangalore, Mumbai, Pune, Kochi, Jaipur, Ahmedabad, and Delhi with a total 2,334 rooms. The company planned to open five new hotels in 2013, and eight new hotels in the following year.

Hathway Cable and Datacom Ltd.

Hathway Cable and Datacom Ltd, promoted by the Raheja Group, is one of the largest multisystem operator and cable television and broadband service provider in India. The company decided to demerge its broadband business to a wholly owned subsidiary, Hathway Pvt. Ltd, with the objective to accelerate value creation for the shareholders of the company.

Agreement between ONGC and Rajasthan Government for Gas Supply

ONGC and Rajasthan State Government signed gas sales and purchase agreement with the terms as follows:

- ONGC was to supply 1.5 m standard cubic meter gas per day from its share of PannaMukta Tapti JV, and
- Gas was to be supplied for 300 MW power plant in Dholpur.

ONGC Videsh Ltd and British Petroleum Donation of Helmets to Students and Teachers

ONGC Videsh Ltd and the British Petroleum agreed in October 2004 to donate 900 helmets to students and teachers of Lang Throng Primary School in Hanoi. This was with the objective to make a positive and meaningful contribution to community and to improve road safety awareness among school children and their parents.

Public Enterprise Agreed for Social Religious Projects

ONGC, a leading public enterprise, agreed for global compact-initiatives projects for the construction of

- A charitable hospital—R K Mission, Sevashram
- Sri Aurobindo Ashram, Noida
- R K Mission of Culture

Another community development project related to adoption of six villages in Tripura by the state enterprise with the objective to provide basic amenities like sufficient power supply, standard education, health service, surface communication, and eco-friendly habitation.

Paltana Power Project in Tripura

A 750 MW gas-based power project was approved to meet the power demands of Tripura and adjoining states where there is a potential demand. The project got forest and environment clearance in October 2005. Tripura state, NBCC, and ONGC are the partners to the project.

The term "Paltana" is a Bengali word to mean "to change."

Furniture Manufacturing Unit by a Japanese Company

Japanese housing and building materials trading firm Sumitomo has bought a 26 percent stake in India's Spacewood for $14 million (Rs. 91 crores). This would give Sumitomo Forestry an entry into India's high-margin furniture segment. Sumitomo and Spacewood would jointly set up a facility for the production of pre-hung doors and they have plans to have 50 retail outlets and gross sales of Rs. 50 crores in the next 3 years (*Source: Economic Times* October 8, 2015).

Ikea, Swedish Furniture Retailer

Considering that home segment is currently dominated by carpenters, and three-fourth of the furniture industry in India is controlled by stand-alone stores and carpenters, there is a major shift toward readymade furniture products. Ikea, a Swedish furniture, is planning to setup furniture production unit in India. Ikea bought land in 2015 in Hyderabad for its first India outlet and plans to open 25 stores by 2025.

Brief Case Examples

Tata Motors and AirAsia Planned to Set Up Joint Venture to Make and Sell Tata Vehicles in South-East Asia

Tata Motors and AirAsia entered into JV to jointly build low-cost vehicles drawn from the stable of Tata Motors Ltd in Malaysia for sale in that country and other markets.

The vehicles proposed to be sold by the JV were Nano, billed as the world's cheapest car, and light commercial vehicles such as the Ace, Magic, and Winger.

The proposed JV would enhance the global footprint of Tata Motors, which had a strong presence in Europe after its acquisition of Jaguar Land Rover in 2008.

Tata had capacity to manufacture at its plant at Sanad in Gujarat 20,000 Nano cars per month of which half was lying idle as the present sale is in the range of 5,000 to 7,000 units.

The Tata group, a salt-to-software conglomerate had traditionally envisaged big-ticket industrial projects and built them from scratch like it did with its steel and automobiles business. Even when the group considered an entry into services, it built businesses such as financial services and information technology without a partner. With this proposed JV, Tata was willing to share management control and even cede this a JV partner.

CHAPTER 2

Project Life Cycle

After having gone through this chapter, you should be able to
- Understand various phases of a project—its beginning and end, and also stages in between;
- Appreciate examples of some projects

Key Terms: Project Life Cycle, Identification, Formulation, Appraisal, Selection, Implementation, Feasibility Report, Commercial Appraisal, Economic Appraisal

As discussed earlier, a project has a beginning and an end, and the project has a path from origin to completion. These stages for the project path indicate the work breakdown structure, a hierarchical subdivision of work. It is also known as project life cycle which is a subdivision of the scope of work[1] into various stages, each representing sequential phase of work. To put it in simple words, a building construction project has the following phases as:

- Concept and initial phase
- Design and development phase
- Implementation or construction phase
- Commissioning and handover phase

The project life cycle normally has a "*Stretched-S*" pattern of *slow–rapid–slow* progress toward the project goal in common. Figure 2.1 shows

---

[1]Kathryn N. Wells and Timothy J. Kloppenborg. *Project Management Essentials*, Business Expert Press, LLC (2014) pp. 53–55.

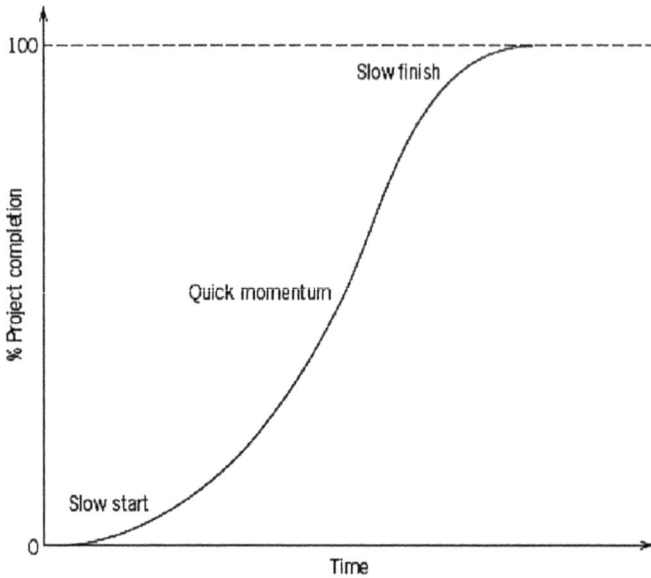

Figure 2.1 Project life cycle—Stretched-"S" Pattern

Source: Meredith Jack R and Samuel Mantel J.

the progressive stages of a project and the changing levels of resources deployed.[2]

These stages involve varied time and efforts. For example, implementation or construction phase, which involves planning, scheduling, monitoring, and control, requires relatively more time and effort as compared to other phases of conception, selection, and evaluation (see Figure 2.2).

To quote PMBOK, "because projects are unique and involve a certain degree of risk, companies performing projects will generally subdivide their projects into several project phases to provide better management control. Collectively these project phases are called the project life cycle."[3]

As such, the project life cycle is of importance to a project manager as he/she has to plan resources for each phase and also has to design a

---

[2]Meredith Jack R. and Samuel Mantel J., *Project Management: A Managerial Approach* (Wiley India Eighth Ed). p.18.

[3]Rory Burke, *Project Management: Planning and Control Techniques* (Wiley India Fourth Ed. 2010) p.28.

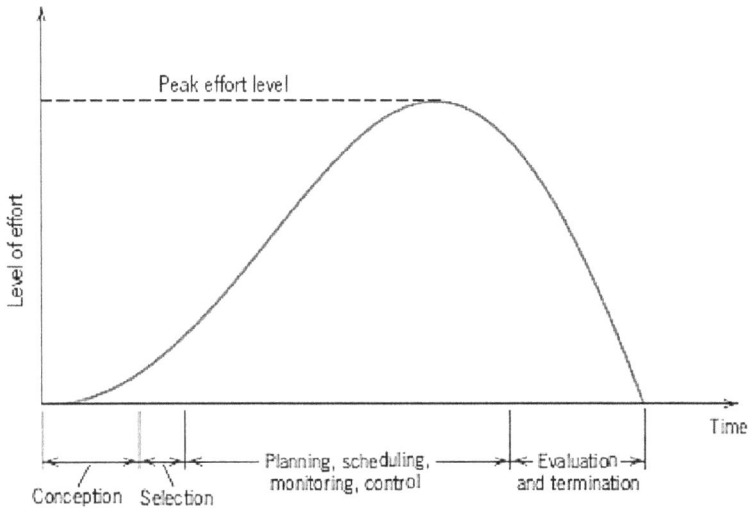

Figure 2.2 Project phases: time and effort level

Source: Meredith Jack R and Samuel Mantel J.

control system. Various phases of a project with which a project manager and/or stakeholders are concerned are

- Project identification
- Project formulation→Feasibility report
- Project appraisal
- Project selection
- Project implementation
- Project evaluation

The above phases though sequential may overlap at times.
These phases are briefly illustrated below.

Project Identification

This is a stage of project conceptualization, given objectives and resources at command. The project is to be identified after analysis of the following:

- Environment scanning: Acquaint with the environment, prevailing regulatory framework, accessibility and availability of utility services, and various inputs required.

- Economic and tax factors analysis: Assess threats and opportunities by analyzing economic policy relating foreign collaboration, export incentives, or tax incentives.
- Industrial policy and regulatory framework examination: Assess possible areas of growth and concern and also availability of backward region incentives.

For the above exercise, the following two could be the alternative bases for project identification:

- "Source" basis: Availability of raw materials, inputs, and other facilities
- "Destination" basis: Output or demand potentials, or market potential

To stay ahead you must have your next idea waiting in the wings

Rosabeth Moss Canter

Project Formulation

Having identified investment opportunities, a project report called Feasibility Report containing detailed information about the project is prepared. Preparation of a feasibility report requires the following:

Project rationale or its justification: Will there be market for the product or the service produced? This would necessitate taking up the exercise of forecasting of demand and supply of the product or service from existing as well as forthcoming industrial units, both domestic as well as international.

Feasibility report also contains details about technology, location, size, inputs specification, or cost estimates or financial requirements. Various aspects of feasibility report are detailed in the next chapter and are the basis of project appraisal.

Project Appraisal

Having gathered information regarding the project, the next stage relates to the analysis of the same to see the feasibility or viability of the project or to see whether the project conforms to the project objectives. Such examination would entail analysis as follows:

- Are technical parameters realistic and optimistic?
- Commercial analysis to determine product specification, market plan, and organization structure and break-even analysis. Are these realistic and attainable?
- Are financial costs and returns properly estimated?
- Is project financially viable?
- Whether project meets social profitability requirements?
- Various techniques of project appraisal are discussed in Chapters 4 and 5.

Project appraisal can be from the view point of promoter or those interested in financial aspects of a project, normally called *commercial appraisal*; or be a macro-level exercise from the point of view of government or regulatory bodies who are also interested in the social impact of the project, which is called *economic appraisal. Commercial* and *economic* appraisals are illustrated below:

Commercial appraisal	Economic appraisal
○ A micro-level exercise ○ For a commercial enterprise ○ Covers purely financial inputs and outputs ○ To arrive at commercial viability of investment proposal, i.e., its profitability or its return ○ For example, for a highway project, the contractor would be interested in commercial aspects of the project, i.e., financial viability or expected profit or loss	○ A macro-level exercise ○ For an economy or society to arrive at economic benefits or costs of a project ○ Besides financial inputs and outputs, also considers social benefits and social costs ○ Taxes and subsidies are treated as transfer payments; for economic costs or prices consider shadow prices ○ Used by national or global institutions or regulatory bodies involved in policy making, like Planning Commission or World Bank ○ For example, for a highway project, the state government or Planning Commission would be interested to ascertain, besides financial aspects, the social aspects of the project. This would include increase in traffic and transport of goods or impact of pollution and employment. These are macro-level effects

Project Selection

After having examined various aspects contained in the feasibility report, it leads to the selection of a project. Thus project appraisal is the basis of making a rational choice of a project. While selecting a project, its objectives and constraints are considered. In other words, project selection is a decision making situation.

Always keep the larger picture in mind while making a decision

Decisions determine destiny

Project Implementation

Having selected a project, steps initiated for its execution are

- To determine sequence of activities by following PERT/CPM network techniques and
- To assess the availability and requirement of resources and time frame for various activities.

This would require planning for various resources so as to ensure completion of the project with minimum cost as per laid down objectives. Project planning lays down the activities, resources, budget, and timeline(s) for the project. This effort, which begins early in the project life cycle, results in the creation of a complete plan, the Project Plan (PP).

*Actions speak louder than words **Anonymous***

*Actions are the insipid reflections of your motives **Anonymous***

The Project Plan (PP) documents (viz., the work breakdown structure—WBS, etc.) how the project will be managed and controlled from an element by element to the delivered whole. It lays out the detailed work plans for both administrative and technical tasks. For each project task, the PP documents what is to be done, by whom, with what funds, when, how (processes to be used), and interdependencies. It also lays down the sequence of activities which can be sequential and independent; the latter ones are also called parallel tasks. The Project Plan should include the purpose and overview of the project, task descriptions, resources and budget allocated to each task, deliverables, and project schedule. It should also include a budget plan that estimates annual/monthly costs and identifies where funds will come from, a project organization, as well as roles and responsibilities relative to project execution. In general, the PP is the "how to" guide for managing the project's execution, and as such it should properly be gone through and approved by all the participants (lenders, promoters, etc.) in the project.

Gantt Charts[4] are useful tools for analyzing, planning, and controlling large/complex multistage projects. Gantt Charts are drawn up using the following steps:

i. List all Activities/Tasks in the Plan.
ii. Plot the Tasks onto the Plan: list all tasks on Y-axis and draw each task as a horizontal bar on X-axis, with the length of the bar being proportional to the length of the estimated time the task will take. Above each task bar, show the estimated time taken to complete the task.
iii. Schedule the Tasks/Activities on a fresh sheet in such a manner that sequential activities are carried out in the desired sequence, for example, dig the ground, lay foundations, begin construction.

The Project Planning (PP) thus includes the steps that will be taken to monitor and control the project as a whole. In short, the PP defines the tasks and schedule for the project and the processes that will be followed to produce the deliverables. Once the project is underway, how can you track progress against the plan? When should you start to worry that the project is veering off track? Is the project on track as long as cost and schedule are meeting the plan?

---

[4]Kathryn N. Wells and Timothy J. Kloppenborg, *Project Management Essentials.* Business Expert Press, LLC (2014) pp. 53–55.

Project Evaluation

This is a soul-searching step to see whichever project has been selected and is being implemented, whether it is conforming to the organization objectives or is as per the plan, or whether it requires mid-course correction and modification. In other words, looking back and comparing actual performance with projected performance. For the purpose, there is a need to have a feedback loop mechanism to

- ascertain project progress
- ascertain achievements against targets
- workout and analyze project cost and time over-run

The feedback would provide inputs for further work on the project under implementation or for similar projects in future.

Instances for Discussion

Hennes and Mauritz AB (H&M) Entry into Indian Market

Hennes and Mauritz AB (H&M), Swedish fashion retailer, planned to open wholly owned stores in India; this followed Indian government's efforts to open the retail sector to foreign investors, allowing 100 percent foreign direct investment (FDI) in single-brand retail and upto 51 percent in supermarket chains and other multi-brand stores.

H&M operated six brands—H&M, COS, Monki, Weekday, Cheap Monday, and Other Stories—via 2,800 stores in 48 countries. It already sourced materials from India for its global operations and this would increase once it launched its stores in India. It was viewed that "it will bring a lot to India, not just customer offering, but also investment in stores, recruitment and increased sourcing." H&M had planned to start with a few stores and would expand heavily over time.

India was viewed as a huge market with apparel, accounting for 6 percent of India's consumption expenditure which was likely to grow four-fold over the next decade, with an estimated consumption expenditure of $225 billion (around Rs.12.4 trillion at present) in 2020.

Other foreign retailers entering India included, Swedish retailer furniture maker Ikea, British footwear maker Pavers, French sports goods retailer Decathlon, and American watchmaker Fossil Inc.

Case Studies

Computerization and Networking of India Post—Plans for Solar Power Backup

India Post planned to provide a solar power backup for its computer systems once computerization and networking all its branches across the country was complete. As such each of its office would get solar panels to ensure the network works even when there was no power.

India Post had 1.55 lakh post offices and all of them would be networked. It was to ensure that system worked uninterruptedly even when there was no power supply and beneficiaries of solar security scheme got payments.

The networking and IT induction program was estimated to cost Rs. 4,700 crores and was estimated to be completed by March 2014. A pilot project was planned to be launched in Srikakulam (Andhra Pradesh).

India Post planned to begin work on the country's fourth Automated Mail Processing Centre in Hyderabad in April 2013; the other centers were to be located at Delhi, Mumbai, and Kolkata.

The Rs.60 crore center, coming up near the international airport at Shamshabad, could sort 30,000 mails every hour. This was expected to reduce time to deliver the mails. "Using powerful scanners and IT solutions, the machines sort out the mail after reading pin-codes and other details in the address area as the mail travels on the conveyor belts."

The India Post delivered 1.75 crores of letters, 2.7 lakhs of parcels, and 1.9 crores money orders every day.

The government planned to set up the National Institute of Electronics and Information Technology Centre at Srikakulam with an outlay of Rs. 50 crores. The center would offer short-term courses in information technology.

(*Source: Business Line* April 2, 2013).

Kochi Port Terminal Development

The Kochi Port had proposed to develop the terminal exclusively to handle coal and fertilizer at the existing berths at Ernakulam Wharf, which were underutilized following the shifting of container terminal operations to Vallarpadam.

Though five firms had responded initially, none of them finally put in their bids as the rates fixed by TAMP for coal handling was said to be too low.

It was reported that the rates fixed by TAMP at Kochi were at Rs. 106.24 per ton while in Vizag, the rate was Rs. 158.98. The rate at Mormugao Port was Rs. 183 and rates for the two terminals of Tuticorin were at Rs. 135.32 and Rs. 113.72 per ton, respectively.

It was also reported that the rates fixed for Kochi were too low and it would be difficult to attract potential bidders for the project.

Thereafter, the port management proposed to increase the draft at these berths to 14.5 m so that the port can attract larger vessels, which would make the port more economical for users.

The development of deep berths to handle coal and fertilizer with rail connectivity would help units not only in Kerala but also in western Tamil Nadu.

The port was already doing dredging at Vallarpadam to create a draft of 14.5 m. This work could be extended to Ernakulam Wharf and additional investment would be only about Rs. 25 crores. Once it was developed, Kochi would certainly emerge as the only major port with deep drafted berths to handle coal.

The feasibility report of the project suggested taking up the project on BOT basis at an estimated cost of Rs. 250 crores. It recommended developing a mechanized general cargo terminal with a total optimal capacity of 8.72 MTPA comprising a coal handling facility and finished fertilizer handling facility of 0.42 MTPA capacity.

(*Source: Business Line* April 2, 2013)

Computerization Services for Government Schools in Maharashtra

IL&FS Education, Core Education and Technologies, and Birla ShlokaEdutech were selected for a Rs. 900 crore project to provide computerization services to 5,000 government schools in key districts of Maharashtra. Payout of Rs. 17.9 lakhs was fixed for each school.

The three companies were given the contract for the supply of computers (and related accessories), education software, and other management systems over a 5-year period. This was the third phase of ICT@ schools scheme being implemented by the central government in partnership with states and union territories across the country.

BOOT Model

The contracts were structured on a build, own, operate, and transfer (BOOT) model, as per that the vendors would have to finance the upfront capital expenses required for providing computerization services. Seven other companies, including large players such as NIIT, Aptech, Educomp, and Everonn, had evinced interest in the project. However, the selected three companies emerged as the lowest bidders.

IL&FSEducation & Technology Services would receive Rs. 458 crores for the implementation in 2,560 schools of Nasik, Aurangabad, Amravati, Nagpur, and Latur regions.

Core Education had been selected for 1,500 schools in Mumbai, Greater Mumbai, Navi Mumbai, and Pune. And it would collect Rs. 284 crores over the 5-year period.

Similarly, the BSE-listed Birla ShlokaEdutech would provide IT services in 850 schools of Kolhapur region for an overall consideration of Rs. 152 crores. The company planned to start providing services to the schools in Kolhapur by August 2013. The contract provided a provision of payments by the directorate every 6 months.

Launched by the Human Resources Development (HRD) Ministry in 2004, the ICT@schools scheme aimed to provide computer education to students of secondary and higher secondary government and government-aided schools. In Maharashtra, the first phase of the scheme covered 500 schools (in 2007 to 2008), while the second phase covered 2,500 schools (2011 to 2012).

Hewlett Packard Split into Two Companies

Hewlett Packard an engineering-driven company founded more than 75 years ago in a garage not far from Stanford University split into two in October 2015 after year of planning. A 500-person team inside HP had done more than 300,000 tests of its systems to see they worked right, built 75,000 new ways to interface with its computers, and cloned 2,800 applications to use in one company or another.

One of the split companies would be HP which would largely consist of personal computers and printers. The other, Hewlett Packard Enterprise, or HPE, would sell the computer servers, data storage networking, software, and consulting services that would run a modern company. Each company was expected to have annual revenue of about $5 billion and would be among America's 50 largest public companies.

Neither of the two new companies would have the standing as one of the most innovative operations in the world that the old HP enjoyed for decades. However, the people who would run the new companies argued that might not be a bad thing. HP for years had endured a sort of corporate existential crisis—a company trying to change with the times while trying to hold on to the past and managing to do neither well.

More important for the future of both new companies were the plans that Meg Whiteman seemed to have worked on since she took over at HP in 2011. Whiteman was of the view that "we have to recognize how much technology has changed and change with that." As such, change was considered as the norm among the old tech giants. In the immediate past Dell announced a deal to purchase EMC, a maker of data storage equipment and software for $67 billion. Lexmark, a competitor to HP's printer business, had hired Goldman to explore alternatives to its beleaguered life as a public company. And IBM had reported declining revenues for 14 consecutive quarters.

(*Source: Economic Times* November 2, 2015)

CHAPTER 3

Project Formulation

After having gone through this chapter, you should be able to

- Oversee contents of feasibility report
- Understand technical aspects of a project
- Appreciate managerial aspects of a project
- Identify the commercial details of a project
  - Analyze project rationale
  - Estimate project cost
  - Estimate project operating cost
  - Understand project operating revenues
  - Estimate project profit, that is, excess of revenues over cost
- Appreciate financial aspects of a project
- View economic aspects of a project
- Appreciate examples of some projects and project management practice

Key Terms: Project cost, operating cost, Project Revenue, Cash inflows, Cash outflows, Financial Ratios, Discount rate

Having identified a project, preparation of the project report is an important task of project management. For example, when we approach a bank for financial assistance, the first thing a banker asks is have you brought the project details? He is referring to the feasibility report of the project for which financial assistance is being sought. Banks and regulatory bodies like Planning Commission normally prescribe the details expected in a feasibility report. The feasibility report is the basis of appraisal by banks or regulatory bodies having stake in the project. In other words, feasibility report is a comprehensive and systematic compilation of data relating to various aspects of a project, namely,

- Technical aspects
- Managerial aspects
- Commercial aspects
- Financial aspects
- Economic aspects

The above aspects are not sequential and at times overlap. These aspects are detailed below.

Technical Aspects

This section lays down details regarding

- Technology to be adopted: Is it indigenous or foreign, has it been used earlier in some other project, and what is the experience of the same?
- Manufacturing process: What process is planned so as to understand its cost and other implications?
- Location of the project: Land availability including for township, so as to see its impact on regional development or entitlement of subsidy, if any.
- Availability of utility services, other services, and manpower.
- Environment: Existing in terms of its effects on population, water, land, air, and flora and fauna.
- Equipment and construction requirements: Size and type required and capacity utilization.
- Transport requirements for bringing in of the raw materials and other inputs and also outward movement of the goods produced.
- Phasing of construction and production as it would have impact on financial requirement and also on the goods produced.

Managerial Aspects

Human resources are the soul of the project, and success of a project to an extent depends upon effectiveness of human resources. For example, of two projects of similar size, one is more successful purely because of its effective or result-oriented human resources. It all depends upon the management, their background, professional qualification, and experience and also arrangements for development for human resource; for example, in an agriculture project, does the management have expertise in agriculture or do they plan to have human resources with that background. Banks also examine the credit worthiness of the entrepreneur. Besides his financial standing or soundness, the bank also analyses whether he has defaulted payment in the past. Banks these days attach greater importance to the managerial aspects and have behavioral workshop with the management. Such details of behavioral aspects are beyond the scope of this book.

Commercial Aspects

It relates to details covering setting of the project, justification in terms of marketing of its products, project cost, cost of operations, operating revenues, and its profitability. Various areas relating to commercial aspects include

Project Rationale: What is the Justification of the Project?

What are the demand and supply estimates for the product/service for future years? Demand forecast is carried out for the future years in terms of existing level of demand as well as demand both for domestic markets and for export markets to be tapped in future due to changing economic scenario. Similarly, supply is estimated in terms of the existing manufacturers and also the new expected establishments, both within the country and abroad. With liberalization and deregulations, in contrast to regulated economy, the aspect of demand–supply estimates has become a complex task as geographical boundaries no longer exist as exports and imports from the foreign markets, many a times, are freely allowed.

As such, such estimates should indicate that the demand outstrip supply and the product produced will have market. Many a time efforts are made to create demand for the product. Such examples are given below:

- Deploying students to go to various stores asking for a particular brand of toothpaste; this was simultaneously advertised on TV, before it was launched in the markets.
- Inserting a matrimonial column in a newspaper, "Wanted a groom having the qualities of a hero of a particular novel," that pushed the sale of that novel.

Estimate Cost of the Project

Project cost estimate should be realistic considering future needs and it includes

- Fixed assets including costs of land, civil works and buildings, equipment and machinery, engineering services, and in-plant infrastructure
- Outside plant infrastructure, like township
- Start-up costs or trial run cost
- Working capital
- Interest during construction period

The above are normally one-time costs and as such are nonrecurring. However, project construction may spread over a number of years, or the project may be in various phases; in that case, the above costs may be spread over various years. Cost elements of a project are illustrated in Box 1. Following **principles** for the project cost are relevant:

i. Cost comprises of all expenses *related* to the project and incurred to bring it in *working condition*, that is, the condition it is intended.

    For example, cost of an automobile purchased which is intended to be driven would include all cost *related* to the car and incurred up to the stage of *bringing it in a state* that it can be driven on the road. Accordingly, road tax, car insurance, and registration charges would be included in the cost of a car as these are required before the car is driven on the road. However, any expense incurred on learning how to drive the car or toward driving license fee would not be included in the cost of the car, as these are not *related* to the car.

Similarly, cost of computer purchased for the office would include its purchased price, cartage, insurance, and installation expenses as these have to be incurred to bring the computer into operating stage.

Expenses incurred on trial run or preliminary expenses incurred for setting up of the project are included in the project cost. For example, as a part of the setting up of the project, two engineers were invited for the trial run or for pretest which involved a cost of Rs. 300 lakhs. But that pretest yielded some output valued at Rs. 50 lakhs. Accordingly, the net cost of trial run of Rs. 250 lakhs would be included in the project cost.

Box 1

Project cost includes—as an illustration:

Land and building: Site development; township

- Plant and machinery
- Furniture and fixture
- Office equipment
- Hardware
- Software
- Railway siding
- Livestock
- Intangibles: License, patents
- Preliminary expenses
- Working capital: Margin
- Interest during construction period
- Contingencies

   ii. All expenses incurred *after* the project has been brought into working condition are not included in the project cost.

  iii. Financing costs, like interest, related to the project and incurred up to the stage of bringing into working condition are included. However, interest incurred after the project is operationalized or interest paid in general not specifically for the project in question is not included in the project cost.

  iv. Administrative and other general expenses *related* to the project are included in the project cost, if these are specifically attributable to the project.

Ascertain Cost of Production

This cost relates to carrying out manufacturing operations and would depend upon the level of operations and capacity utilization which may vary over the years. As such, this cost is recurring one and is necessary for carrying out the operations. Elements of operating cost are illustrated in Box 2.

Box 2

Operating Cost Elements: An Illustration

- Materials
- Expenses on components acquired
- Manpower expenses
- Utilities
- Repairs and maintenance
- Travel
- Rent, rates, and taxes
- Publicity
- Security expenses
- Legal expenses
- Depreciation and amortization
- Interest on borrowings

For example, a production unit having a capacity to produce 1,000 units per day is operating at 60 percent in the first 2 years and at 80 percent thereafter; various operating expenses, as illustrated in Box 2, will be estimated at 60 percent level for the first 2 years and at 80 percent level thereafter.

Estimate Project Revenues

This would depend upon the estimated number of units to be sold and the expected selling price for the future years However, for social and community development projects, minimum economic benefits or reduction in operating costs is proxy for the projected revenues.

For example, for highways projects: "avoidable costs," that is, reduction in vehicles' operating costs and road maintenance are proxy for revenues estimates.

Similarly, for irrigation projects, expected increase in agriculture production after irrigation is the basis for revenue estimation; and for agriculture projects, market value of estimated increase in output is proxy for revenues.

For public utilities like power or waterworks, administered prices are the basis of revenue estimates. In case, benefits to consumers exceed administered price, the value of economic benefits is the revenue. Similarly, for social and community development projects like education, health, and population planning, opportunity cost for rendering of the services is the basis of revenue estimation.

Surplus (Deficit) from Operations—Year Wise

From the estimates of operating costs and revenues, surplus or deficit is calculated for different years. In other words, surplus is estimated revenues (d) *minus* estimated operating costs (c) for different years. In commercial terms, surplus (or deficit) is called profit (or loss).

Financial Aspects

Arranging finances for a project and also deciding about mix of various sources are important tasks for the project manager. Traditionally, sources of funds include owners' fund, popularly known as equity and debt. Promoters' contribution is supplemented with funds raised from the public. Banks and financial institutions contribution is primarily in the form of debt, but this have different variants each having different implications. In addition, the funds may be for a short period or long period. The following two principles should be the guiding factors for finalizing finances for a project:

- Match funds requirements for a project with the funds availability. Avoid using short-term funds for the project requirements which are normally of long-term nature.
- Have a capital mix so as to minimize financing cost and the restrictive covenants attached.

(*Details of finances of a project are discussed in Chapter 6 Vol. 2*).

In addition, banks adopt various financial techniques to analyze a project. These include

- Financial ratios:
  - Profitability
  - Liquidity
  - Solvency
  - Activity
- Break-even level calculation: It is the level of operation with no-profit-no-loss or a situation where
- Total revenues = Total costs, that is, no-profit-no-loss
     For that purpose, look for a level of capacity utilization, where
  - Total revenue equals total cost or
  - The year in which the break-even level is attained, earlier the better

(*These aspects are beyond the purview of the text.*)

Further, infrastructure projects have different characteristics and private sector is being involved in developing and managing such projects. Development of Indira Gandhi International Airport in Delhi by involving GMR is a recent example. Private sector is involved through approaches like BOOT/BOT/BOLT. Under these approaches, the private agency has three roles:

- Designer or constructor
- Financer
- Operator

Securitization is another approach of financing projects.

(Details regarding infrastructure projects development and their financing are discussed in Vol. II Chapters 8 and 9.)

Economic Aspects

In this section, we look at the economics of a project, that is, to estimate its cash inflows and cash outflows for future years and to analyze these cash flows. In other words, it has following two aspects:

i. Cash flows estimation: That is, estimate cash outflows and cash inflows over the life of the project. Cash outflows are outflows on account of project cost and are normally at the beginning of the project and may occur in later years also. Cash inflows are annual cash inflows arising from sales after meeting operating cash expenses over the years.

ii. Appraisal techniques: Various techniques are used to analyze the inflows and outflows.

A word of caution while analyzing the cash flows:

- There is no one *Best Technique.*
- Every technique has some strong points.

In that respect, management judgment is supreme for appraisal and for deciding about the project.

(Appraisal techniques are discussed in the next chapter.)

Cash Flows Estimation

- Cash outflows are project cost as discussed above.
- Cash inflows are estimated on profit after tax (PAT) basis. However, for macro projects or for socio/community development projects where there is no profit element, profit before tax is the basis of cash inflows.
- In other words, **cash inflows are PAT + depreciation + interest**

where

- ○ Depreciation is a part of project cost; it is a noncash expense or is merely a book entry and does not involve cash payment
- ○ interest charge being a "Transfer Payment" is not considered as an expense while estimating cash inflows

For cash flows estimation see the following illustrations:

Illustration 3.1

Cash flows calculation (uniform revenues and no tax)

- Project cost: Rs.30,000
- Finances: Equity 10,000; 10% debt 20,000, i.e., project outflows = Rs. 30,000

Operations:

- Sales revenue Rs. 40,000 pa; depreciation Rs. 5,000 pa, and interest expenses Rs.2,000 pa
- Project life 5 years
- No gestation period

Year I	Revenue II Rs.	Operation and maintenance (O&M) expenses III Rs.	Interest IV Rs.	Depreciation V Rs.	Total expenses VI (III + IV + V) Rs.	Surplus VII (II − VI) Rs.	Cash inflows VIII (VII + IV + V) Rs.
1	40,000	30,000	2,000	5,000	37,000	3,000	10,000
2	40,000	30,000	2,000	5,000	37,000	3,000	10,000
3	40,000	30,000	2,000	5,000	37,000	3,000	10,000
4	40,000	30,000	2,000	5,000	37,000	3,000	10,000
5	40,000	30,000	2,000	5,000	37,000	3,000	10,000

Illustration 3.2

Cash flows calculation (increasing revenues and corporate tax 40%)

- Project cost: Rs. 25,000, i.e., project outflows = Rs. 25,000
- Finances: Equity 10,000 and debt 15,000

Operations:

- Increasing sales revenue
- Uniform depreciation Rs. 4,000 pa
- Interest charges Rs. 1,200 pa
- Life 5 years
- No gestation period

Years	I	II	III	IV	V
A) Sales Rs.	39,000	47,000	55,000	55,000	55,000
Expenses: b1) RM, fuel, utilities	15,000	18,000	22,000	22,000	22,000
b2) Manpower	9,800	14,000	18,000	18,000	18,000
b3) Others	1,000	1,800	1,800	1,800	1,800
b4) Depreciation#	4,000	4,000	4,000	4,000	4,000
b5) Interest#	1,200	1,200	1,200	1,200	1,200
B) Total expenses	31,000	39,000	47,000	47,000	47,000
C) Profit (A − B)	8,000	8,000	8,000	8,000	8,000
D) Tax 40%	3,200	3,200	3,200	3,200	3,200
E) Net profit (PAT)#	4,800	4,800	4,800	4,800	4,800
F) Cash inflows# (E + b4 + b5)	10,000	10,000	10,000	10,000	10,000

Instances for Discussion

Mahindra Stake in Ssangyong Unit

Mahindra and Mahindra planned to raise its holdings in Ssangyong Motor Co. to 72.85% in a 80 billion Korean won ($73.73 million) investment.

Mahindra, India's biggest sports utility vehicle manufacturer, would subscribe to preferential shares issued by Ssangyong. This was to facilitate new product development and to strengthen the South Korean company's financials. The payment was expected in May 2013.

Real Estate Project: Macquarie Infrastructure and Real Assets

Macquarie Infrastructure and Real Assets (MIRA), an arm of Australia's Macquarie Group Limited, plans to invest in real estate projects in India. The company manages over $100 billion of assets. The company in India, Macquarie Infrastructure and Real Assets (India) Pvt. Ltd, would be managed by R. K. Narayan who was earlier a consultant with real estate investment firm AevitasProperty Partners and also served as the chief operating officer at Infinite India Investment Pvt. Ltd.

MIRA is planning to invest in luxury residential projects jointly with Tata Housing Development Co Ltd, a subsidiary of Tata Sons.

MIRA is a large infrastructure asset manager globally and also has portfolio in real estate agriculture and power across. Its real estate portfolio includes 20 retail, commercial, residential, and industrial properties in China, Mexico, and Australia. (*Source: Mint,* October 27, 2015).

Brief Case Studies
Tata Sampann: Consumer Products and Food Division

Tata Chemicals Ltd, maker of branded salt and pulses, announced its entry into spices business, and all its consumer products and food segment, such as I-ShaktiBesan (gram flour) and pulses, would come under the Tata Sampann brand except iconic Tata Salt. This was with the objective to treble revenues from the consumer product business to Rs. 5,000 crores in the next 4 years. The move is to focus on quality assurance and play in the mass-market space and better value proposition. The company had been selling pulses since 2010 under the I-Shakti brand and the same network would be used for spices and products that would be launched in the future.

It has planned to launch single-use sachets of spices (five small sachets of 20 gm each in a 100 gm packet). Tata Chemicals had a strong presence in fertilizers, chemicals, crop protection chemicals, specialty fertilizers, and branded food products and food additives.

The overall food market in India is estimated at about Rs. 6 trillion crores; the packaged food market was estimated at Rs. 20 billion in 2014; the spices market in India is estimated at Rs. 40,000 crores, of which just 15 percent is branded.

For sources of pulses, the Tata Chemicals has engaged 150,000 farmers, an initiative led by Rallis India Ltd, a Tata Enterprise. This was to monitor the entire supply chain—from farm to consumer to ensure quality. Tata Chemicals planned to expand its retail footprint to about 2.5 million outlets from the current 1.43 million.

The other fast moving consumer goods (FMCG) providers include ITC Ltd, Hindustan Unilever Ltd; and Swiss packaged food company Nestle India Co. Their retail outlets include 4.3, 6.3, and 4.5 million, respectively.

Sanad Hospital in Riyadh, Saudi Arabia

Aster DM Healthcare, a company owned by Dubai-based Indian billionaire Dr. Azad Moopen, acquired from a Saudi partner, in October 2015, 57 percent stake in Sanad Hospital in Riyadh, Saudi Arabia, for Rs. 1,600 crores, taking its total stake to 97 percent. Earlier 40 percent stake was acquired in December 2011. Thus with the recent acquisition of 57 percent stake, Aster DM Healthcare had become a majority stakeholder.

The deal closed after the necessary clearance from the Saudi Arabia General Investment Authority (SAGIA), the body that takes foreign investment-related decisions in the kingdom. The Kingdom of Saudi Arabia allows 100 percent foreign investment in hospitals provided a player can prove that he would bring in capital and expertise.

With the above acquisition, Rs. 420 crore Aster's footprint in West Asia extended to all six Gulf Cooperation Council (GCC) countries and Jordan. The healthcare company that operated through a portfolio of hospitals, clinics, and pharmacies had five green field projects underway in GCC, one hospital in Qatar and four in the United Arab Emirates.

Under the company's two-pronged growth approach, India where the company ran eight hospitals continued to be a focus market for Aster. Further, the company had invested Rs. 550 crores in Aster Medicity in Kochi and was putting in nearly Rs. 230 crores in Aster CMI Hospitals in Bengaluru. As per the policy of the company, "In India we see an opportunity in both mid and long term. Our focus will be to build a position of strength in South and West. And we also see medical tourism as an interesting opportunity."

The company which started Indian operation in 2001 had three hospitals in Kerala (Calicut, Kottakal, Kochi), two in Maharashtra (Pune, Kolhapur), two in Telangana (Hyderabad), and one in Karnataka (Bengaluru). As per the policy, "In India and abroad we like to follow model that involves taking a majority stake. It allows us accountability and also flexibility to do various things." As such, Aster had a bed capacity of 2,022 in India compared to 517 in GCC.

Dr. Azad Moopen was awarded Padma Shri and belongs to the set of Maayai entrepreneurs like M. A. Yussuff Ali, Ravi Pillai, Sunny Varkey, and P. N.C. Menon. (*Source: Economic Times,* October 12, 2015).

Plaza Cables Ltd: Estimation of investment outlay in a machine

Plaza Cables Ltd (PCL) is contemplating to replace its old equipment by a new sophisticated one costing Rs. 10 crores plus 8 percent sales tax. PCL will be getting a discount of 10 percent on the equipment cost from the supplier in Bengaluru. The transportation and insurance will cost Rs 1 lakh each. In addition, the installation will cost another Rs. 5 lakhs. The equipment being sophisticated one, there will be production trials to ensure proper adjustments; the trial runs will cost Rs. 10 lakhs of which 4 lakhs will be realized from the produce of production trials.

The new equipment would necessitate an increase in minimum level of inventory by Rs. 15 lakhs. In addition, the old machine having a book value of Rs. 40 lakhs is estimated to be sold for Rs. 20 lakhs, the company is entitled to save @ 20 percent on capital loss on account of the sale of old equipment.

Bright Motors Company: Estimation of Cash inflows for a Project

Bright Motor Company (BMC) is planning for a project to add a new production unit at Manesar, Haryana. Mr. Mohan Rai, member of the project team is involved with the task of estimation of cash inflows from the project operation. Production operations for the project are estimated as under:

Capacity utilization	60%
Sales pa in units in crores	6.00
Sales (crore Rs.)	180
Operation expenses (crore Rs.)	
Raw material and components	100
Manpower cost	20
Factory supervision cash cost	10
Administrative and other expenses	10
Marketing and publicity expenses	5
Gross profit (PBDIT)	35
Depreciation	10
Profit before interest and tax (PBIT)	25
Interest on borrowings	5
Profit before tax (PBT)	20
Tax 25%	5
Profit after tax	15

Requirements:

Estimate cash inflows from the project

HIsmelt Plant in Australia Relocated to China and not to Jindal Steel and Power Ltd (JSPL), Orissa

Managements of Jindal Steel and Power Ltd (JSPL), Orissa, and Rio Tinto, Australia, had agreed on August 5, 2011, to relocate the existing HIsmelt plant from Kwinana in Australia to India at JSPL's existing facility at Angul in Orissa. The relocated plant was to be fully owned by JSPL, and the Indian company and Rio Tinto were to work together to further develop and market the technology.

As against the above arrangement, the HIsmelt technology plant in Australia had been dismantled and sent to China and not to JSPL in Orissa on the understanding that the Chinese company Molong had more urgent need for the technology. Molong's normal supplies of liquid pig iron were stopped for environmental reasons and was not allowed to build conventional blast furnaces. For environmental reasons, HIsmelt was the only technology capable of producing liquid pig iron at the required capacity and environmental standard. It is viewed that China leapt ahead of Jindal and got HIsmelt plant.

Further, it was argued that bringing the plant to India involved "too many changes" and so it was relocated to a Chinese company as "a pilot plant."

After the pilot run in China, JSPL would build a plant at its Angul site with the HIsmelt technology with a capacity of 1 or 1.2 mt and this was envisaged for construction in 2015 with the production starting the next year.

HIsmelt—short for high-intensity smelting—is a technology owned by Rio Tinto and is said to be ideal for India. JSPL could directly use iron ore fines and noncoking coal, abundantly available in India, and it is said to be environmentally friendly and more economical than traditional methods.

CHAPTER 4

Project Appraisal

After going through this chapter, you should be able to
- Identify various techniques of project appraisal
- Appreciate the difference between traditional and modern techniques
- Understand the importance of discounting of cash flows under modern techniques
- Appreciate the differences and commonalities in the modern techniques
- Oversee the computation of IRR
- Appreciate the limitations of IRR/BCR/NPV
- Understand the modified PBP and modified IRR
- Appreciate examples of some projects and project management practice

---

Key Terms: Appraisal techniques, Cash flows, Discounting, Payback Period, NPV, Benefit Cost Ratio, IRR, Modified Payback period, Modified IRR, Cost of Capital

Having formulated the project proposal giving all details of the project as discussed in the previous chapter, let us examine the viability of the project, that is, its financial viability. This is a two-step exercise:

i. Estimation of cash flows—inflows and outflows (*refer Illustrations 3.1 & 3.2 in the previous chapter*)
   Cash outflows are project cost, while cash inflows are PAT + depreciation + interest.

ii. Evaluation of cash flows for various projects: This is with an objective to select a project that is economically viable and yields maximum return on investment. For the purpose, various techniques are used for analysis of the cash flows.

A word of caution while using various techniques:

- There is no one best technique.
- Every technique has some strong point.

In that respect, management judgment is supreme, and there is no substitute for decision making to select a project.

Man is the principal syllable in management

C. T. McKenzie

Various techniques[1] for project appraisal techniques include

- Ranking by inspection
- Accounting rate of return (ARR)
- Payback period (PBP)
- Net present value (NPV)
- Benefit–cost ratio (BCR) or Profitability Index (PI)
- Adjusted payback period (PBP Adj.)
- Internal rate of return (IRR)
- Modified internal rate of return (MIRR)
- Economic rate of return (ERR)

First three techniques are termed as *traditional techniques*, while the others are called *modern techniques*. The last one is a technique for economic appraisal for macro-level projects.

The above techniques are illustrated in the following pages.

---

[1]Refer to Chapter 4, pp. 44–46 of Information Systems Project Management by David Olson, Business Expert Press, LLC (2015).

Exhibit 4.1

Ranking by Inspection

Project	Year	Outflow Rs.	Inflows Rs.	Net Inflows Rs.	Ranking by Inspection
A	1	20,000	10,000	10,000	2
	2	—	10,000	10,000	
	3	—	—	—	
B	1	20,000	10,000	10,000	1
	2	—	10,000	10,000	
	3	—	970	970	
C	1	20,000	10,000	10,000	2
	2	—	6,000	6,000	
	2	—	12,000	12,000	
D	1	20,000	15,000	5,000	1
	2	—	12,000	12,000	
	3	—	6,000	6,000	

Ranking by Inspection

Projects are ranked by looking at the inflows and outflows for various projects. Such ranking is merely by personal judgment and is not a systematic one. To illustrate, of the four projects in Exhibit 4.1, ranking is by comparing the inflows and outflows and as such between the two projects A and B, rankings are 2,1 and between projects C and D rankings are 2, 1.

Such ranking is crude one, is on personal judgment, and is not systematic and not followed by banks and financial institutions.

Accounting Rate of Return (ARR)

Accounting profits are used as the basis of appraisal. Profits of a project are related with the investment of the project and a project with higher profit rate is selected. It is calculated as

ARR = Profit for the year/investment $\times$ 100

where profit = PAT;

investment is average (Avg.) investment, that is, investment adjusted for annual depreciation.

So,

ARR = Avg. PAT/Avg. investment × 100

where Avg. profit is the average of profits at the beginning and end of the yearly profit for the project and Avg. investment is investment adjusted for depreciation for the year.

ARR for a project is compared with the cost of capital or the borrowing rate to ascertain whether the project is acceptable. If the ARR is more than cost of capital, the project is considered feasible.

Cost of capital is the cost of funds deployed in the project; it is the minimum return expected from the project. In case of different sources of financing such as equity and debt, it is the average cost for the various sources. As discussed latter, it is also known as the discount rate or hurdle rate.
Decision Rules:

- *ARR = Avg. PAT/Avg. investment × 100*
- *Accept a project when ARR > cost of capital*

Among number of projects having ARR greater than cost of capital, accept a project with the highest ARR.

ARR has the following **positive** points:

+ Easy to understand
+ Considers profits for the entire life of project

ARR has the following negative points:

—Based on accounting information and not on cash flows
—Does not consider time value of money

The value of data is directly related to their timeliness

—Not conceptually sound as PAT is after interest, depreciation, and tax, while investment comprises of equity as well as debt, so there is inconsistency in its computation

ARR is a good accounting measure but not a technique for project appraisal.

For illustrations in the previous chapter, ARR will be as under:

Illustration I (for Illustration 3.1)
Avg. profit/Avg. investment
1/5 (3,000 + 3,000 + 3,000 + 3,000 + 3,000)/
1/6 (30,000 + 25,000, + 20,000 + 15,000 + 10,000 + 5,000) = 17.14%

Illustration II (for illustration 3.2)
ARR = Avg. PAT/Avg. investment = 32%

Payback Period (PBP)

Payback period represents period within which annual inflows from the project are sufficient to recover investment.
So,

PBP = Investment/annual inflows
where annual inflows are uniform over the years.

Where inflows are not uniform over the years, cumulative cash flows are calculated to see the years within which cumulative inflows are adequate to recover investment.

Decision Rule:
Accept a project with lowest payback period

For Illustrations in the previous chapter, PBP will be as under:

- Illustration I = 3 years
- Illustration II = 2.5 years

PBP has the following **strong** points:

+ Simple and commonly used
+ Considers projects of shorter recovery period and so risk is taken care of
+ Emphasizes on liquidity
+ A useful, quick, preliminary screening device if sophisticated analysis is worth

PBP suffers from the following **shortcomings**:

—Considers only a part of inflows
—Ignores time value of money
—Not a profitability measure

As mentioned earlier, ARR and PBP are also known as traditional methods of appraisal
(*refer illustrations in Chapter 5*).

Discounted Cash Flows Methods

These are methods which discount inflows and outflows for time as they occur at different time intervals. These methods are

- Net present value (NPV)
- Benefit–cost ratio (BCR) or Profitability Index (PI)
- Adjusted payback period (PBP Adj.)
- Internal rate of return (IRR)
- Modified IRR (MIRR)

The above methods are also known as modern methods of project appraisal.

Before we discuss the modern methods of appraisal, let us discuss, in brief, the concept of discounting and time value of money.

Discounted Cash Flows: Principles

- *Discounting of cash flows is also known as ascertainment of present value of the cash flows expected over the years; **it is reciprocal of compounding**.*

  To illustrate:

  Consider compounding of cash inflows for time @10%, as under:

  0 yr-------. . .. .-.. -- → yr 1 -------. . .. .---- yr 2

  Rs. 100 = ---becomes ... Rs. 110 = ---becomes--- Rs. 121 at the end of year 2.

  As Rs. 100 deposited in a bank in year "0" becomes Rs. 110 at the end of year "1," it also becomes Rs. 121 at the end of year "2."

- *Looking the other way, discounted cash flows for time at 10% are as under:*

  Rs. 121 at the end of year 2 = Rs.110 at the end of year 1, or Rs. 100 at year 0

  Rs. 100 = ←---. . .. . --------Rs. 110 = ←. . .. . ..----------- Rs. 121

  where 10% is assumed as discount rate

- As mentioned earlier, discount rate is the cost of raising funds for the project. It is the average cost of raising funds from different sources, and is also known as *"Cost of Capital" or "cutoff rate"*

Time Value of Money: Principles

- *"Compounding"* is a process of ascertaining value in future (FV) from the present value (PV) at a certain rate,

    that is, ascertainment of value in second year from the value in year"0" at a certain rate

- Whereas *"Discounting" is a process of ascertaining PV from future value (FV) at a certain rate,*

    that is, ascertain value at present from the value in future years

- *So discounting is the reciprocal of compounding*

Time Value of Money

  Time is a great teacher but unfortunately it kills all its pupils

- *"Time"* is important in time value analysis

Time Line:

---------. . .---------. . . . .*---------. . .*---------. . . . .*----. . . . .

0   1yr   2yr   3 yr   4yr   5yr

Rs. 100 today at time "0" becomes 110 at time yr 1 end,
   i.e., {100 + 10% (100)} = 110; or
{100 × (1 + 0.10)}, or
becomes 121 at time yr2 end, i.e., {110 + 10% (110)} = 121;
   or {110 × (1 + 0.10)}, or
becomes 133.1 at time yr 3 end, i.e., {121 + 10% (121)} = 133.1;
   or {121 × (1 + 0.10)}

Having discussed the concept of discounting because of time, let us discuss the discounting methods of project appraisal.

Net Present Value (NPV)

NPV == PV of inflows *less* PV of outflows, in rupee terms, that is,

NPV == PV (I) – PV (O)
where

- NPV is net present value,
- PV (I) is present value of inflows, and
- PV (O) is present value of outflows, at a certain rate.

Decision Rule → Go--No-Go

- *Go, when NPV is ("positive" or +)*
- *No-Go, when NPV is ("negative" or −)*
- *Prefer a project with highest NPV*

(See Illustrations IV and V in the next chapter.)

Benefit–Cost Ratio (BCR) or Profitability Index (PI)
In computation,

BCR = PV (I)/PV (O), a ratio

where PV(I) = present value of inflows at a discount rate and

PV(O) = present value of outflows at a discount rate

BCR is similar to NPV and uses the same information, where NPV is in rupees, while BCR is a ratio.

Decision Rule:

- *Reject a project with BC ratio < 1*
- *Accept a project with BC ratio > 1*
- *Prefer a project with higher BC ratio >1*

Computation of NPV and BCR is illustrated for two projects A and B in Exhibit 4.2.

Exhibit 4.2

	Project A	Project B
Project cost	Rs. 25,000	Rs. 25,000
Inflows	Uniform Rs. 10,000 pa	Rs. 5,000 pa for first 4 years and Rs. 25,000 in the fifth year
Project life	5 years	5 years
Discount rate	10%	10%

Year ↓	Project A	Project B	PV Factor	Project A PV	Project B PV
0	(25,000)	(25,000)	1.00	(25,000)	(25,000)
1	10,000	5,000	0.909	9,090	4,545
2	10,000	5,000	0.826	8,260	4,130
3	10,000	5,000	0.751	7,510	3,755
4	10,000	5,000	0.683	6,830	3,415
5	10,000	25,000	0.621	6,210	15,525
Total	50,000	45,000	3.790	37,900	31,370
Payback	2.5 yr	4.2 yr	PV (O)00E8	(25,000)	(25,000)
NPV 10%				12,900	6,370
BC 10%				1.51	1.25
IRR%				29.05	17.6
PB Adj.				3.02 yr	4.59 yr
MIRR				20%	16%

Outflows reflected by () –   Inflows reflected by +

Of the two projects A and B, at discount rate of 10% Project A has positive NPV greater than that of Project B so accept Project A.

Similarly Project A has greater BCR so accept Project A.

NPV and BCR—Comparison—illustrated below

	NPV	**BC Ratio**
Information needed:	Inflows	Inflows
	Outflows	Outflows
	Life	Life
	Discount rate	Discount rate
Information obtained	NPV (Rs.)	Ratio
Decision rule	Go–No-Go	Go–No-Go
	No-Go when NPV (—) → Reject	No-Go when, BCR < 1 → Reject
	Go When NPV (+) → Accept Prefer a project with highest (+) NPV	Go when, BCR > 1 → Accept Prefer a project with highest BCR
where discount rate is the cost of raising funds.		

From the comparison of NPV and BCR for the four projects in Exhibit 4.3, one finds that

- NPV and BCR both give the same result when projects are of equal size.

Exhibit 4.3

NPV and BCR Computation—Illustration where Projects are of equal size of Rs. 25,000 each

	Project A	Project B	Project C	Project D
PV (I)	37,900	31,370	25,000	23,000
PV (O)	25,000	25,000	25,000	25,000
NPV	12,900	6,370	0	(−) 2,000
BCR	1.51	1.25	1.00	0.92
Project ranking NPV	First rank	Second rank	Indifferent	Reject
Project ranking BCR	First rank	Second rank	Indifferent	Reject

Comparison of NPV and BCR when projects are of different sizes, that is, projects A, B, C, and D have size of Rs. 25,000 each while project E has a size of Rs. 75,000, is illustrated in Exhibit 4.4.

Decision Rule:

- **Use BCR**
- **Select a project with highest BCR**

Exhibit 4.4

NPV and BCR Computation—Illustration where Projects are of Unequal size

	Project A	Project B	Project C	Project D	Project E
PV (I)	37,900	31,370	25,000	23,000	90,000
PV (O)	25,000	25,000	25,000	25,000	75,000
NPV	12,900	6,370	0	(−) 2,000	15,000
BCR	1.51	1.25	1.00	0.925	1.2
Project ranking NPV	Second rank	Third rank	Indifferent	Reject	First rank
Project ranking BCR	First rank	Second rank	Indifferent	Reject	Third rank
Ranking by NPV gives deceptive results		So go by BCR			

Internal Rate of Return (IRR)

Internal rate of return (IRR) is the rate of return from the project after discounting of cash flows, where present value of cash inflows equals the present value of cash outflows.

To calculate IRR:

**Ascertain discount rate by discounting of cash flows, such that
PV (I) = PV (O) or BCR = 1 or NPV = 0, i.e.,
PV (I) – PV (O) == 0; or
BCR = PV (I)/PV (O) = 1
The discount rate ascertained is the IRR.**

IRR Computation: IRR can be calculated by

- use of computer: ascertain a rate where discounted inflows = discounted outflows, or
- iteration process: calculate PV inflows and PV outflows at various discount rates by using PV Table,

where $\sum PV(I) = \sum PV(O)$, a cumbersome process

- interpolation formula, discussed below

IRR—Thumb Rule:
IRR is the reciprocal of payback period under certain conditions as

- Inflows are uniform over the years and
- Project is of long life

IRR—Interpolation Formula

IRR lies between two rates, that is, between a low rate (L) and a high rate (H), such that

at "*L*" discount rate, NPV is *Positive (+) and*

at "*H*" discount rate, NPV is *Negative (–)*

So, IRR = L + [NPV (L)/Abs. (PV (I)L – PV (I) H] ×(H – L)

For illustration in Exhibit 4.2 above, at "L" 10% and "H" 30%, interpolation formula

= 10% + [12,900/37,900 – 24,360] × (30 – 10)

= 10 + 19.05 = 29.05

Comparison of NPV, BCR, and IRR is illustrated in Exhibit 4.5.

Exhibit 4.5

Comparison of NPV, BCR, and IRR

	NPV	BC Ratio	IRR
Information needed	Inflows	Inflows	Inflows
	Outflows	Outflows	Outflows
	Life	Life	Life
	Discount rate	Discount rate	?

	NPV	**BC Ratio**	**IRR**
Information obtained=>	NPV (Rs.)	BC ratio	Discount rate where PV(I) = PV (O)
Decision rule	NPV (–) → Reject NPV (+) → Accept Prefer a project with highest (+) NPV	BCR < 1 → Reject BCR > 1 → Accept Prefer a project with highest BCR	IRR < COC → Reject IRR > COC → Accept Prefer a project with highest IRR being greater than COC

NPV/BCR/IRR—Limitations:

The discounting methods discussed above although commonly used have some limitations as these are based on certain assumptions. These include:

- Discount rate is assumed to be constant throughout the project.
- Cash flows are assumed to occur at equally spread interval at the end of the year.
- These are static methods at the time of analysis.
- *Cash inflows during the intermittent years are **Reinvested**.*
- *Reinvestment rate is assumed to be **the discount rate followed**.*
- In addition, for IRR, there is a situation of
- *Multiple IRR (see Exhibit 5.3 . . . . . in the next chapter)*

Adjusted Payback Period (PBP Adj.)

PBP discussed above does not discount cash flows for time; to overcome this weak point, PBP is calculated for cash flows adjusted for time and this is known as adjusted payback period (PBP Adj.).

So PBP Adj. is the period within which discounted inflows are sufficient to cover discounted outflows.

PBP Adjusted Computation:

For illustration in Exhibit 4.2 (discounting at 10%)

Project: A = 3.02 years

Project B = 4.59 years

Modified Internal Rate of Return (MIRR)

Discounted cash flow methods (discussed above) namely, NPV, BCR, and IRR have several limitations, one such limitation being the reinvestment rate, that is, inflows during the intermittent period are reinvested at the rate of discount. MIRR is a discounted cash flow method which takes care of this limitation. It calculates rate of discount at the terminal date equating discounted inflows and outflows and is called MIRR.

One today is worth two tomorrows and if you have something to do tomorrow do it today
MIRR Calculation: Steps

1. Calculate present value (PV) of outflows involved, i.e., present value of project cost using the discount rate.
2. Calculate the terminal value (TV) of the cash inflows expected from the project using the discount rate. This results in a single stream of cash inflows in the terminal year.
3. Calculate the rate of discount which equates the present value (PV) of outflows (Step 1 above) with the terminal value of inflows (Step 2 above).

The rate so calculated equates the PV of outflows in the zeroth year with the terminal value of cash inflows and is the MIRR.

Illustrations

Illustration 4.1: Computation of IRR

Johnson Watch Co. is considering an investment proposal as under:

Year	Cash flows Rs.
0	(136,000)
1	30,000
2	40,000
3	60,000
4	30,000
5	20,000

NPV 10% = PV (I)10% − PV (O)10% == 138,280 − 136,000 = Rs. 2,280

NPV 12% = PV (I)12% − PV (O)12% == 131,810 − 136,000 = Rs. 26,410

So IRR lies between 10% and 12%

By interpolation

IRR == 10% + {2,280/(138,280 − 131,810)} × (12 − 10) = 10.711%

MIRR calculation for Illustration 4.1:

MIRR Calculation Steps :

Step 1. PV of outflows Rs. 136,000

Step 2. Compounded value of inflows at the terminal year 5th at 8%

1.	30,000	1.3605	40,815
2.	40,000	1.2597	50,388
3.	60,000	1.1664	69,984
4.	30,000	1.0800	32,400
5.	20,000	1.0000	20,000
	Total		213,587

Step 3. MIRR is obtained as:

136,000 == 213,587 / (1 + MIRR)

136,000 / 213,587 == 0.6367428 which lies between 9 % and 10% in

Table PV interest factor at five years

So MIRR is 9.5%

Illustration 4.2

For Anderson Sons, given outflows in the first 2 years and inflows in the subsequent years are given as:

Year	Cash flows	Discount Factor 10%	Discount Factor 20%	PV 10%	PV 20%
0	−120	1.0	1.0	−120	−120
1	−80	0.909	0.833	−72.72	−66.64
2	20	0.826	0.694	16.52	13.88

(Continued)

Illustration 4.2 (Continued)

Year	Cash flows	Discount Factor 10%	Discount Factor 20%	PV 10%	PV 20%
3	60	0.751	0.579	45.06	34.74
4	80	0.683	0.432	54.64	34.56
5	100	0.621	0.402	62.10	40.20
6	120	0.564	0.335	67.68	40.20
	Σ PV (I)			246.00	163.58
	Σ PV (O)			192.72	186.64
	NPV			53.28	−23.06

So IRR lies between 10% and 20%

By interpolation IRR $= 10 + 53.28/\{(246 - 163.58)\} \times (20 - 10)$
$$= 16.64\,\%$$

MIRR calculations:

Step 1. PV of outflows at 15% = 120 + 80 (0.870) = 189.6

Step 2. Compounded value of inflows at terminal year 6 at 15%

Year	Inflows	Compound value of inflows factor	Compound value
2	20	1.749	34.98
3	60	1.521	91.26
4	80	1.322	105.76
5	100	1.150	115.00
6	120	1.000	120.00
Total			467.00

Step 3 MIRR is obtained as

189.6 == 467/(1 + MIRR)

189/467 == 0.4059957 which lies between 19% and 20% in PV

Table for interest factor at 5 years

So MIRR is 19.5%

Case Studies

Water Supply Project of a City Municipality—Part I

Municipal Corporation of a Western State in India is planning to set up fully automatic water works for its newly developed colonies. Order for the plant and equipment costing Rs. 170 crores plus sales tax 5% was placed on June 20, 2000. Freight and insurance in transit was likely to cost Rs. 2 crores. The land was provided by the local government at a concessional price and construction together with land costed Rs. 25 crores. The plant was received on December 12, 2000, and was operational after installation on April 1, 2001, the installation charges being Rs. 18 crores.

Funds for the project were arranged through government grant of Rs. 200 crores and 12% Rs. 100 crores bank borrowings.

The commissioner of the Municipal Corporation is in charge of the project and is responsible for its planning, commissioning, and operations, with monthly expenses of Rs. 8 lakhs. In addition, a group of employees were provided training in project operations and the training cost was Rs. 25 lakhs.

A consultant, expert in water treatment plant, was hired with a consultation fee of 5 percent of the equipment cost.

Ascertain project cost from the above information.

Water Supply Project of a City Municipality—Part II

The project was expected to provide water services to households with a monthly billing of Rs. 20 crores. As per normal practice, 1 month billing was estimated to remain outstanding. In addition, to ensure regular supplies, stock of raw materials and supplies was to be maintained for 4-week requirements. Raw materials and supplies accounted for 30 percent of the billing.

Will the above information affect the project cost estimated in Part I above?

Water Supply Project of a City Municipality—Part III

Operational details of the project for the first 20 years were as under:
• Annual billing Rs. 240 crores
• Material and supplies cost: 30 percent of billing

- Manpower cost including Commissioner: Rs. 5 crores per annum for first 2 years and Rs. 7 crores for the subsequent 18 years
- Depreciation and interest: Rs. 30 crores per annum for the first 5 years and Rs. 25 for the subsequent 15 years
- Other expenses: Rs 2. crores per annum
- Realizable value of equipment, building, and working capital at the end of 20 years is estimated to be Rs. 30 crores

Requirements:

- Ascertain: annual revenue cost, annual profit, project cost, annual cash flows
- Analyze the viability of the project and give your recommendations
- In case financing of the project has to be redrawn, what alternative sources would you suggest indicating their cost implications?

CHAPTER 5

Project Appraisal, Price-Level Changes, Social Cost–Benefit Analysis

---

After having gone through this chapter, you should be able to
- Appreciate project appraisal in complex situations
- Understand comparison of NPV and IRR
- Overview situations of conflicting results of NPV and IRR and issue of multiple IRRs
- Illustrate situations of independent projects and mutually exclusive projects
- Appreciate the need for adjustment of price-level changes
- Understand the concept of social cost–benefit analysis
- Appreciate adjustment for risk in the project appraisal process
- Overview examples of some projects and project management practices

---

Key Terms: Reinvestment Rate, Capital Rationing, Mutually Exclusive Project, Independent Project, Multiple IRR, Annualized Benefit, Sensitivity Analysis, Price-Level Changes, Social Cost–Benefit Analysis, Shadow Price

Having discussed project appraisal techniques in the previous chapter, the present this chapter discusses comparison of appraisal techniques and presents certain situations where these techniques give conflicting results or a situation of multiple IRR. Situations of independent projects and of mutually exclusive projects are also discussed. Further, issues relating to price-level changes, adjustment for risk, social cost–benefit, and qualitative factors for project management are illustrated.[1]

Comparison of Various Appraisal Techniques

Project appraisal techniques have common points in respect of information required and also of points of analysis (see Exhibits 4.4 and 4.5 of Chapter 4). Let us compare two techniques, NPV and IRR.

NPV and IRR Relationship

As discussed, both NPV and IRR take into consideration time value of money and adjust for differences in the timings of cash flows. Both the methods assume reinvestment of cash inflows during the life of the project and the reinvestment rate for NPV calculation is assumed to be the discount rate itself (i.e., 10% for Project A in Exhibit 5.1), while for IRR calculation the reinvestment rate assumed is the IRR itself. There are, of course, situations, where the assumption of the reinvestment rate being IRR itself does not hold true in reality. On the other hand, such assumption holds true for NPV as the discount rate followed is the cost of capital, and as such NPV is conceptually better.

Figure 5.1 illustrates the relationship between NPV and IRR. The figure plots NPV for Projects A and B, against the discount rates used to evaluate the cash flows. Note that for the Project A, at 10% discount rate, NPV is Rs. 12,900, while at 29.05% discount rate, NPV is 0 and that is the IRR. As against this, for Project B, at 10% discount rate, the NPV is Rs. 6,370, while NPV is 0 at 17.6% and that is the IRR (see Figure 5.1 and Exhibit 5.1).

There are situations where NPV and IRR give conflicting results. What can be those situations? When does it so happen? How to overcome such a problem? A situation of conflicting results is presented in Exhibit 5.2, with two projects P and Q.

As per Exhibit 5.2, NPV and PI (benefit–cost ratio) are higher for project P, as compared to those for project Q, accordingly project P

---

[1]Based on Chapter 11 of The Practice of Management Accounting by Sastry K S and Dhameja Nand, (Wheeler Publishing 1995).

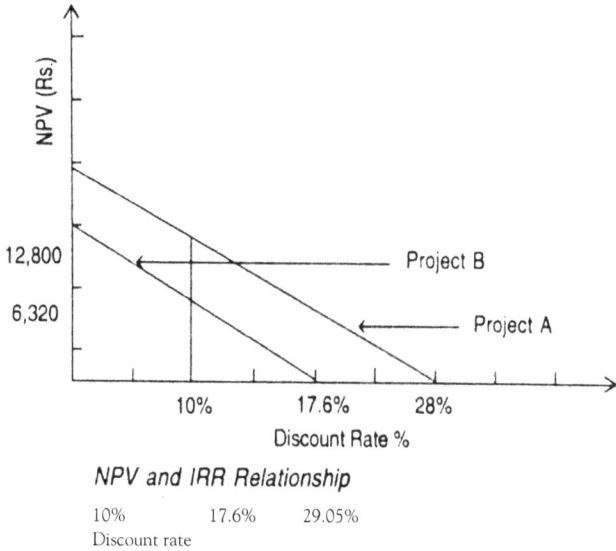

Figure 5.1 **NPV and IRR relationship**

appears to be preferable than project *Q*. As mentioned earlier, this is on the assumptions that the inflows during the intermittent period are reinvested at the rate of discount followed (i.e., 10%).

On the other hand, IRR for project *Q* is higher as against that for project P and project *Q* should be preferred over project *P*. It is on the assumption that the inflows during the life of the project are reinvested at the IRR (i.e., 37.56% for project *Q* and 27.3% for project *P*). It raises a point: can cash inflows be reinvested at 27% in project *P* and at 37% in project *Q*?

The assumption for NPV that inflows would be reinvested at the discount rate of 10% for both the projects, being nearer to reality, makes NPV conceptually better.

Conditions where IRR and NPV may rank projects differently

- Pattern of cash flows: The cash inflows for one project increase overtime while that of the other decrease, a situation similar to that in Exhibit 5.2.
- Projects have different expected lives.
- Different sizes: Cost of one project is higher than that of the other.

Exhibit 5.1

Two projects of equal size but having different inflows

	Project A	Project B
Project cost	Rs. 25,000	Rs. 25,000
Inflows	Uniform Rs. 10,000 pa	Rs. 5,000 pa first 4 yrs and Rs. 25,000 in the fifth year
Project life	5 yrs	5 yrs
Discount rate	10%	10%

Year ↓	Project A	Project B	PV Factor	Project A PV	Project B PV
0	(25,000)	(25,000)	1.00	(25,000)	(25,000)
1	10,000	5,000	0.909	9,090	4,545
2	10,000	5,000	0.826	8,260	4,130
3	10,000	5,000	0.751	7,510	3,755
4	10,000	5,000	0.683	6,830	3,415
5	10,000	25,000	0.621	6,210	15,525
Total	50,000	45,000	3.790	37,900	31,370
Payback	2.5 yr	4.2 yr	PV (O)→	(25,000)	(25,000)
NPV 10%				12,900	6,370
BC 10%				1.51	1.25
IRR%				29.05	17.6
PB Adj.				3.02 yr	4.59 yr
MIRR				20%	16%

Outflows shown in ( )   Inflows shown without ( )

In Exhibit 5.2, the two projects are of equal size but have different patterns of inflows, increasing for project P and decreasing for project Q, but the analysis shows conflicting results for NPV and IRR. To iterate, it is primarily because of the assumption of reinvestment rate in IRR and NPV. In such cases, we should either modify assumptions of the IRR or use BCR which is conceptually sound. Such modification of IRR is beyond the scope of this book.

Exhibit 5.2

Two projects of equal size but having different patterns of inflows are as:

	Project P	Project Q
Project cost	Rs. 70,000	Rs. 70,000
Life	5yrs	5yrs
Inflows	Increasing over the years	Decreasing over the years
Year ↓	Project P	Project Q
0	(70,000)	(70,000)
1	10,000	50,000
2	20,000	40,000
3	30,000	20,000
4	45,000	10,000
5	60,000	10,000
Total	165,000	130,000
Payback period	3.2 yrs	1.5 yrs
NPV 10%	46,135	36,550
BCR 10%	1.659	1.522
IRR	27.3%	37.56%
PBP Adj.	3.71 yrs	1.44 yrs
MIRR	22%	20%

Situation of Multiple IRR

Further, there are situations we may have two or more IRRs, where NPV is 0. (As mentioned earlier, IRR is the rate of discount where the present value of inflows equals the present value of outflows.) These are situations where there are some cash outflows on the abandonment of the project. For example, Exhibit 5.3 shows Projects A *and* B, where the initial outflows are followed by 1- or 2-year inflows, which are then followed by an outflow.

Such cases are found in natural resource projects. In mining, a bauxite firm is normally required as a part of the contract to restore the landscape after digging out the ore deposits. Similarly, an oil company, as a part of the lease agreement is required to inject water into the underground

reservoir in order to make possible a secondary recovery at such time
when the primary reserves are exhausted.

For Multiple IRR, the conditions required are

- Sum of outflows exceeds or equals the sum of inflows. In other
  words, a situation of multiple IRR arises where the net present
  value is nonlinear as shown in Figure 5.2.
- Number of IRRs will be the number of times there is change in
  algebraic signs.

Taking inflows as positive and outflows as negative, in Exhibit 5.3, for
Project A algebraic signs have changed twice (from negative to positive and
then to negative), so Project A has two IRRs of 25 percent and 400 percent.

Similarly, Project B has three IRRs of 0 percent, 100 percent, and
200 percent.

Though there are several approaches to deal with the situation of multiple IRR, these are considered beyond the purview of this book. However,
the net present value method is adopted for decision making in such cases.

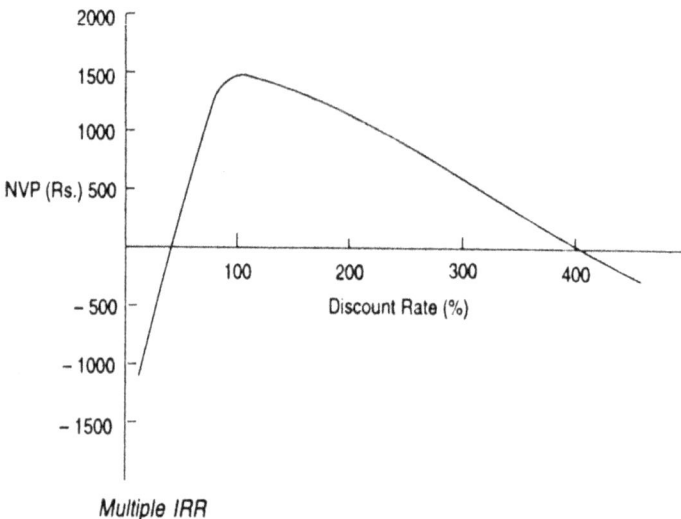

Multiple IRR

Figure 5.2 Situation of multiple IRR

Exhibit 5.3

Multiple IRR

Year ↓	Project A	Project B	Project C
0	− (1,600)	− (1,000)	− (1,000)
1	+ 10,000	+ 6,000	+ 1,400
2	− (10,000)	− (11,000)	+ 100
3		+ 6,000	
IRRs(%)	25 and 400 Two IRRs	0, 100,and 400 Three IRRs	32.5
Multiple IRR: conditions	Sum of outflows ≥ sum of inflows		
No. of IRRs=	No. of times reversal of algebraic signs of inflows and outflows		

In **Exhibit** 5.3, Projects A and B have multiple IRRs as

- in Project A, sum of outflows are greater than sum of inflows
- in Project B, sum of outflows are equal to sum of inflows

Further, number of IRRs = No. of times there is reversal of algebraic signs of inflows and outflows.

Multiple IRR,
where sum of outflows ≥ sum of inflows, and
Number of IRRs = No. of times there is reversal of algebraic signs
of inflows and outflows

Accordingly, in Project A there are two IRRs as 25 percent and 400 percent, while in Project B there are three IRRs as 0 percent, 100 percent, and 400 percent. On the other hand, for Project C, sum of outflows being less than sum of inflows, IRR is 32.5 percent.

Independent Projects and Capital Rationing

As mentioned earlier, where acceptance of one project does not debar the inclusion of the other projects, the situation is one of independent projects. One or more projects can be taken at a time and the availability of funds is the critical factor and it is a situation of capital rationing.

In principle, more projects should be added as long as the marginal revenue is greater than the marginal cost, and to maximize profits they should operate up to a point where the marginal revenue equals the marginal cost. For this purpose marginal revenue is the rate of return earned on successive investments and marginal cost is the cost on successive increments of capital.

Figure 5.3 illustrates that investment up to point $0L_2$, the point where marginal revenue equals marginal cost, is optimal. For investment beyond this point or below this point (i.e., $0L_1$ and $0L_3$), the profit is not maximized.

An enterprise having a number of project proposals is constrained by scarce funds and this gives rise to a situation of capital rationing. The principle of capital rationing is to allocate funds to projects which have a higher return and to reject projects which are not viable. The various steps involved in the finalization of independent projects are summarized as follows:

Step 1   Calculate the Profitability Index (PI) for each of the project proposal.

Step 2   Rank the proposals according to their profitability indices (PIs or BC ratios) in a descending order (from the highest to the lowest).

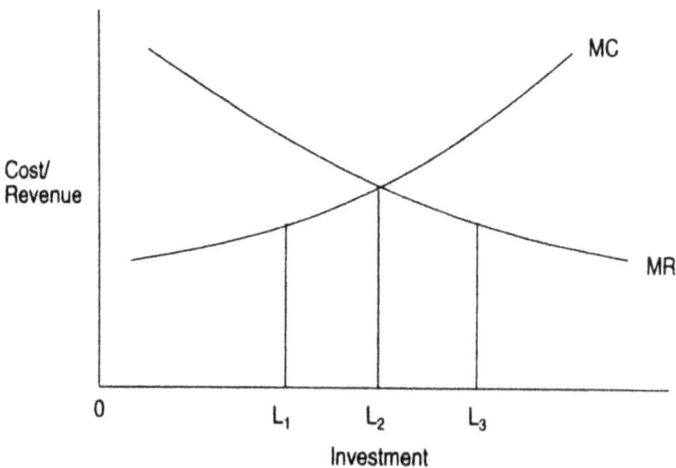

Figure 5.3 Cost/revenue versus investment

Step 3   Reject project proposals having a PI less than unity.

Step 4   Of the remainder, begin with the proposal having the highest PI, proceed down through the list, and accept proposals until the entire available funds have been utilized

(see Exhibits 5.4 and 5.5).

Independent Project and Capital Rationing

M/S Lalbahi & Sons have 10 investment project proposals requiring funds amounting to Rs. 141 lakhs. They have Rs. 60 lakhs available with them. Which of the projects should be accepted? The fund requirement for each project with corresponding PI is given below.

The above case is a situation of capital rationing and would require the following steps:

1. Arrange projects in the descending order of their PI.
2. Reject projects having PI below 1, that is, projects no. 4, 3, and 6.
3. Accept projects with high PI as long as the available Rs. 60 lakhs is utilized.

Exhibit 5.4
Independent Projects and Capital Rationing

Project	Investment (Rs. Lakhs)	Profitability Index (PI)
1	20.00	1.6
2	12.00	1.45
3	23.00	0.78
4	2.00	0.97
5	5.00	1.08
6	2.00	0.63
7	3.00	1.14
8	36.00	1.17
9	11.00	1.25
10	17.00	1.38

Exhibit 5.5

Independent Projects: PI and Fund Allocation

Fund allocated to various projects: A situation of Capital Rationing

Projects	Investment Rs. Lakhs	Cumulative Investment Rs. Lakhs	PI
1	20	20	1.6 ⌐
2	12	32	1.45
10	17	49	1.38
9	11	60	1.25 ⌐
8	36	96	1.17
7	3	99	1.13
5	5	104	1.08
4	2		0.97 Reject⌐
3	23		0.78 Reject
6	2		0.63 Reject⌐

So projects selected are 1, 2, 10, and 9. In case there is a tie, linear programming techniques can be used for allocation and that is beyond the scope of this book.

Mutually Exclusive Projects

These are alternate projects, that is, acceptance of one precludes the acceptance of other projects. Evaluation techniques like NPV, PI, and IRR are adopted to decide about the selection of one project. However, the use of these techniques would depend upon the characteristics of projects in view. For example, in Exhibit 5.1 we concluded that Project A should be preferred over Project B. However, Exhibit 5.2 indicated that NPV and IRR give conflicting results and in such cases, NPV is conceptually better. Situations of mutually exclusive projects could be analyzed under the following two categories:

A) Projects with equal lives, or
B) Projects with unequal lives

A) Projects with Equal Lives: These could be further categorized as

a) Projects of equal lives, having the same size and the same pattern of cash flows

Projects A and B in Exhibit 5.1 have equal lives, the same size and the same pattern of cash flows; NPV or IRR give similar results which are not conflicting.

b) Projects of equal lives, but having unequal size or having a different pattern of cash flows

Projects P and Q in Exhibit 5.2 are of equal lives but different pattern of cash flows and in such cases NPV and IRR give conflicting results, NPV is conceptually better, and NPV or PI can be used for decision making.

How to resolve the conflicting situation?

There are two alternatives to overcome such a situation. The alternatives are

i. To use NPV if projects are of the same size. However, if the projects are of different sizes, PI should be used.

ii. From the cash flows of two projects, determine the difference of cash flows and thus create another project say "R" by subtracting the cash flows of one from that of another (see Exhibit 5.6).

Calculate IRR for the newly created project R. If IRR of the new project R is greater than cost of capital, select the project with the higher cash flows.

To illustrate, Exhibit 5.6 is an extension of Exhibit 5.2 and presents a new project R. This is created by subtracting cash flows for Q project from that of P project (given in Exhibit 5.2).

IRR by Interpolation Formula

$$IRR = [NPV(L)/Abs.(PV(I) - PV(I)H] \times (H - L)])$$
$$IRR = 10\% + \{9,585/(62,465 - 30,250)\} \times (30 - 10) = 15.95\%$$

Assuming that the cost of capital, called cut-off rate, is 15%.

So, Accept Project P.

Decision Rule

Accept *P*, if IRR for *(P – Q)* >cost of capital; since 15.95% > 15%, accept *P*.

Exhibit 5.6

Projects with Equal Lives with different flow pattern

(this is an extension of Exhibit 5.2)

	Project P	Project Q	(P – Q) Project R	at Discount Rates	
0	(70,000)	(70,000)		10%	30%
1	10,000	50,000	(40,000)	(36,360)	(30,760)
2	20,000	40,000	(20,000)	(16,520)	(11,840)
3	30,000	20,000	10,000	7,510	4,550
4	45,000	10,000	35,000	23,905	12,250
5	60,000	10,000	50,000	31,050	13,450
				(52,880)	(42,600)
				62,465	30,250
				9,585	(12,350)

B). *Projects with Unequal Lives*

In case the projects proposed have unequal lives, the following four alternative approaches of analysis are as under:

Approach a) Consider reinvestment opportunities for inflows during the intermittent period of the project and compare the expected reinvestment rate of the shorter duration project with IRR of longer duration project.

Decision Rule

i. If the expected reinvestment rate > IRR of the longer project, prefer the shorter duration project, alternately
ii. If the expected reinvestment rate < IRR of the longer project, prefer the longer project.

Approach b) Add other similar projects so as to equalize the lives for the two projects. NPV can be calculated for the two alternative proposals of 30 years each.

This approach is theoretical one and assumes that opportunity for adding more projects exists and also there is a possibility of reinvestment during the intermittent period. Further the assumptions are nor realistic.

Approach c) Cut off the analysis for the two projects of unequal lives at terminal year that of shorter life project, estimate terminal value of longer project at that terminal date and appraise the two projects by various techniques. This approach though very common requires the estimation of value at the year of termination.

Approach d) Another approach is to annualize the respective cash flows pattern of the alternate projects and select a project having the minimum annualized cost or the maximum annualized gain.

The formula for annualization is

Annualized cost = (Present value of cash flows)/
(present value factor for the given year as ascertained from the Annuity Table)

Decision Rule:

- Select a project with minimum annualized cost or
- Select a project with maximum annualized benefit.

The present value factor is a factor which when applied to the present value amount gives the yearly installment. In other words, present value factor is reciprocal of the PV of the rupee one received over the life of the project at a given rate of interest.

Annualized cost for the Projects A and B is illustrated in Exhibit 5.7.

Project Investment and Risk

Project investment proposals relate to future which is always uncertain. Accordingly estimates of cash flows for a project are not certain. In addition, return from a project is directly related to anticipated risk; greater the risk, higher the return and vice-versa. Different investment proposals

Exhibit 5.7

Annualized Cost of two projects

A company has two alternate proposals requiring initial investment of Rs. 100 lakhs and Rs. 80 lakhs, respectively. They have lives of 10 years and 6 years, respectively.

Their operating cash costs are as under:

	Project A	Project B
Life	10 yrs	6 yrs
Initial investment (Rs. 000)	10,000	8,000
Operating costs (Rs. 000) in years	2,000	2,500
1	2,000	2,500
2	2,000	2,500
3	2,500	3,800
4	2,500	3,800
5	2,500	3,800
6	3,000	
7	3,000	
8	3,000	
9	3,000	
10		
Salvage value (Rs. 000)	1,500 end of tenth year	1,000 end of sixth year

The Annualized Cost is Calculated as under:

	Project A	Project B
Present value of original cost and annual operating costs at 10% (Rs. 000) Less present value of salvage	25,014 (578)	21,316 (565)
Total cost (PV)	24,436	20,750
Annualized cost	(PV of cash flows)/PV of annuity 24,436/6.1446 = 3,976.83	20,750/4.3553 = 4,764.54
Decision rule	Accept project with lowest annualized cost	
	SO ACCEPT PROJECT A	

(More illustrations of mutually exclusive projects are given at the end of the chapter.)

have different levels of risks. Risk refers to the potential variability of returns from investment proposals and the more variable these returns, the greater is the risk. It raises the need to make an adjustment for risk in investment appraisal. A brief description of approaches for the adjustment of risk is given below.

Swings and Roundabout Principle

One method of dealing with risk is to ignore it altogether. It would seem odd to regard this as a method of dealing with risk, but would be sensible if seen from the point that risk is random in its incidence and is likely to cause better than expected results as it is to cause worse than expected. When we aim at a rate of return of say 15 percent, we discover that, on an average, this is what occurs on the "swings and roundabout" principle. In such circumstances, risk can safely be ignored. However, unfortunately, this happy averaging out does not always happen in practice. In most cases we are likely to find that the nature of the risk is such that we may find a project doing substantially worse than expected, but rarely substantially better than expected. Two clear reasons for this are the project manager's enthusiasm to push the project through and the difference between the anticipated capacity utilization and the actual.

Expected Values

Another approach to adjust for risk is that the project manager estimates not one set of cash flows, rather several possible sets of cash flows are estimated with probabilities for each estimate. This method of probability estimate of cash flows for risk adjustment is beyond the scope of this book.

If a man will begin with certainties he will end in doubts

Sir Francis Bacon

Risk-Adjusted Discount Rate

The philosophy of this method is that a project involving risk will be expected to offer a premium in excess of that of a risk-free project. The greater the risk involved in a project, the greater the required premium in return and higher the discount rate used in the project evaluation. Conversely, a lower discount rate is used for less risky projects.

In other words, as risk increases, higher expected returns are required to compensate for the additional risk, and investors trade-off between risk and return. For example, an investor may be indifferent to a risk-free project having a sure return of 5 percent, or to a moderately risky project with a 7 percent return, or to a very risky project with a 15 percent return.

The trade-off between risk and return is made clear in Figure 5.4. The investor is expected to have a *5 percent* risk-free return; with risk, the investor would expect a higher rate of return of 16 percent, the risk measured in terms of coefficient of variance of 1.5. In other words, he is indifferent between risky investment projects of B, C, and D and the risk-free return of *5 percent* from project A.

The risk factor under this method is usually judged by the cash flow pattern of a particular project and thus will remain to be a subjective decision. Second, this method applies a constant risk-adjusted discount rate, which fails to take into account fluctuating degrees of risk throughout the life of the project. Third, it assumes that the cash flows can be reinvested at the risk-adjusted discount rate.

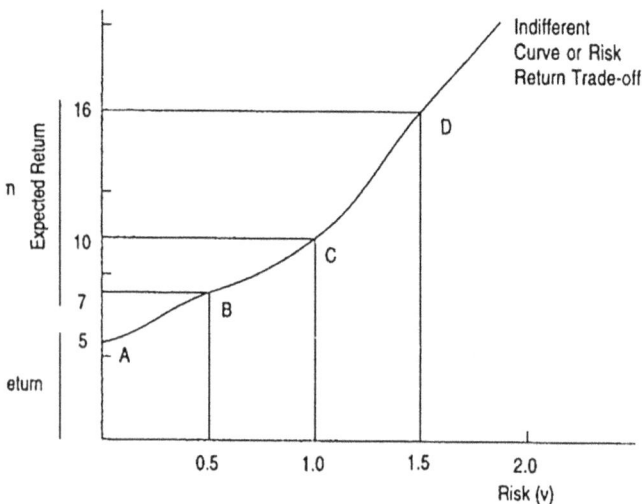

Figure 5.4 Indifferent curve or risk return trade-off

Due to the limitations mentioned above, some suggest adjustment of the cash flows rather than the discount rate. Estimated cash flows are converted into certain cash flows by applying what is known as a "certainty equivalent coefficient," depending on the degree of risk inherent in cash flows. For evaluation purposes, all project cash flows are discounted by a risk-free discount rate.

Certain statistical methods or techniques like standard deviation (called Hillier's model), simulation (called Hertz's model), discrete probabilistic analysis (DPA), and continuous probabilistic analysis (CPA) are used to measure risk; these are beyond the scope of the book.

Sensitivity Analysis

Sensitivity analysis is a way of showing effects of uncertainty by varying the value of the key factors, say sales, price, and costs, and showing the resulting effect on the project. It is a procedure to study the responsiveness of net present values or IRR to variations in one of the cash flow elements like price, sales, and cost and to determine how sensitive a project's return to a change is in a particular value.

Since estimates of cash flows are generally based on a single estimate of factors like selling price, sales volume, and cost of production, sensitivity analysis shows how sensitive is NPV or IRR estimate with the variation in the estimates of various variables.

Sensitivity analysis is derived from the simulation approach and requires the definition of all relevant variables which influence NPV and IRR of the project.

Steps involved in sensitivity analysis are

I. Identifying the critical or sensitive elements of inflows and outflows and
II. Analyzing the effect of variation of such elements on the expected NPV or IRR.

For example, if raw material costs increase by 10 percent or sales fall by 10 percent, or selling price increases by 10 percent, how sensitive would be the return from the project? Thus sensitivity analysis tests the viability of the project under the worst circumstance.

Project Planning and Price-Level Changes

A point can be raised that during inflation when prices are increasing, how to adjust for inflation while planning a project?

Inflation reflects increasing price level and a fall in money value. Inflationary conditions are those where too much money will be chasing too few goods and services, and thus cause a general increase in the prices of goods and services. Inflation distorts cash flow estimates and thus the results of project appraisals. Project appraisal techniques do not automatically take into account the inflationary factor. This necessitates specific inclusion of inflation in project planning and analysis.

Need for adjustment for price-level changes arises, when there is time gap between inflows and outflows and there is inflation during the period. As in a project, investment is made at the beginning and inflows occur over the years in future; and during this period there may have been increase in prices.

Inflation adjustment would depend upon whether cash flows are estimated at constant prices or current prices. If constant prices are used to estimate project cash flows, no separate adjustment needs to be made as constant prices imply that inflation has been taken care of. On the other hand, if cash flows are estimated in terms of current prices, inflationary adjustment becomes necessary. The real difference is the difference between money cash flows and real cash flows. Money cash flows are the actual amounts of money changing hands, whereas real cash flows are the purchasing power equivalents of the actual cash flows. In a world of zero inflation, there would be no need to distinguish between money and real cash flows as they would be identical. Where inflation does exist, there arises a difference between money and real cash flows which necessitates adjustments while evaluating projects.

There are two approaches for adjustment for price-level changes:

a)   Adjust discount rate—so as to include for inflation, that is, add a factor for inflation in the discount rate used. So discount rate would be say, 12 percent (10% without inflation plus 2% for inflation) or

b) Adjust estimated cash flows for price-level changes. Steps required are as follows:

    i. Forecast inflation rates for the coming years

    ii. Adjust annual cash flows on account of inflation estimated above

    iii. Evaluate adjusted cash flows and calculate NPV, BCR, IRR, or PBP Adj.

Illustration: For Project B in Exhibit 5.1 above, cash inflows are adjusted for the estimated inflation rate. These are shown in Exhibit 5.8. These adjusted inflows are appraised by using various techniques, namely, NPV, BCR, and IRR. This is shown in Exhibit 5.9.

Exhibit 5.8

Adjusted Cash flows for Price-Level Changes

(for Project B shown in Exhibit 5.1)

Yr	Inflows	Expected Inflation rate %	Adjusted Inflows	Inflows adjusted
1	5,000	10	$5{,}000 \times (100/110) =$	4,345
2	5,000	11	$5{,}000 \times (100/110)$ $(100/111) =$	4,095
3	5,000	19	$5{,}000 \times (100/110)$ $(100/111)(100/119) =$	3,441
4	5,000	14	$5{,}000 \times (100/110)$ $(100/111)(100/119)$ $(100/114) =$	3,019
5	25,000	16	$25{,}000 \times (100/110)$ $(100/111)(100/119)$ $(100/114)(100/116) =$	13,010

Social Cost–Benefit Analysis for Project Appraisal

Social cost–benefit analysis is essentially an approach to evaluate public investments or investment in social projects. Steps involved in using social cost–benefit analysis while evaluating a project are

Exhibit 5.9

Appraisal of Cash flows adjusted for Price-Level Changes

(for Project B shown in Exhibit 5.1)

	Inflows adjusted for inflation	Discount Factor 10%	Present value of cash flows
0	(25,000)	1.00	(25,000)
1	4,345	0.909	3,950
2	4,095	0.826	3,282
3	3,441	0.751	2,584
4	3,019	0.683	2,062
5	13,010	0.621	8,079
	PBP Adj.	4.7 yrs	
	NPV 10%	25,000 − 19,957 = (−) 5,043	
	BCR 10%	0.798	

a) Listing of the costs (capital, revenue, internal, external, etc.) and benefits of the project over its life span.

b) Quantification of costs and benefits in terms of market value.

c) Applying shadow prices to obtain the social value of each item.

d) Obtaining the net social benefit after discounting the benefit stream with an appropriate social discounting rate. (Basically, either the interest rate prevailing in the market or social opportunity cost of capital as decided by the value judgment of the policy maker. In fact, it needs consideration of how a project will affect the economy and to whom the costs and benefits will accrue. This is often a subject of controversy.)

e) Accepting if the project gives either zero or positive present social value and rejecting if the present social value is negative.

It would be clear from the above steps that it is not that simple to make use of this concept of social cost–benefit analysis. The specific difficulties are

i. In listing *all the benefits* that are likely to accrue because of a particular project
ii. In *measuring* some of the benefits *in economic terms*
iii. In deciding the life of the project
iv. In choosing the appropriate social discount rate
v. In determining the shadow prices

It should also be noted that social cost–benefit analysis is not meant to substitute financial analysis based on market prices. In fact, financial analysis is always the first essential step toward project appraisal. It helps in identifying the micro aspects of costs and benefits associated with a project. However, basing a judgment about the acceptability of a project on financial analysis alone may result in misallocation of economic resources. Hence, financial analysis must be complemented with social cost–benefit analysis, so that the potential acceptability of a project is tied up with economy-wide macro considerations and repercussions.

In short, there are projects which have social implications resulting in certain social benefits or social costs which are not necessarily in financial terms. For example, construction of a road or a bridge may, in addition to monetary costs and benefits, lead to increase in passenger traffic and also commodity traffic which in turn would increase GDP. On the other hand, it may adversely affect the existing employment or add to pollution level. Similarly, automation may increase production and may affect the society by affecting the people employed. These are very common in national-level or macro-level projects and require adjustment while appraising the project for the society or the government.

Social cost–benefit analysis is illustrated for the construction of bridge across River Ganga in Case Exercise and also for State Electricity Board case study at the end of the chapter.

Case Exercises

Case Exercise 5.1: Two projects with unequal lives— Annualized Cost

Asean Co. has two alternate proposals with details as under:

	Project X	Project Y
Project cost (Rs. 000)	20,000	20,000
Project lives	8 years	10 years
Salvage value (Rs. 000)	2,000	2,000
Discount factor	10%	10%

Find annualized cost of both the projects and which project should be selected?

	Project X	Project Y
Present value (PV) factor at the end of project PV of salvage value (Rs. 000)	0.467 20,000 × 0.467 = 934	0.386 2,000 × 0.386 = 772
Remaining cost (Rs. 000)	20,000 − 934 = 19,066	20,000 − 772 = 19,228
USPVF	5.335	6.145
Annualized cost (Rs. 000)	PV of total cost/USPVF 19,066/.5.335 = 3,573	19,228/6.145 = 3,129

Since annualized benefit of Project X is higher, select that project.

Case Exercise 5.2: A Manufacturing Project Situation

Given details:

- Outlay or project cost Rs. 1000,000; life 10 years
- Annual output 20,000 units
- SP per unit Rs. 25
- Cash cost per unit 17.50
- Cash inflows Rs. 150,000 pa (i.e., Rs. 7.5 × 20,000)

Project Appraisal

- Payback period = 6.67 years
- NPV 10% = 10 lakhs − [(6.1446)(150,000)] = Rs. − 78,310
- NPV 8% = 10 lakhs − [(6.7101) (150,000)] = Rs. 6,515
- IRR = 8% + [(6,515)/(1,006,515 − 921,675)] × (10—8)
  = 8% + (6,515/84,840) × 2 = 8.15%
- PBP Adj. 8% = 9.89 years

Case Exercise 5.3: Project to Construct a bridge across River Ganga—Social Cost–Benefit Analysis

The project was to construct a bridge across River Ganga in Eastern Bihar.

Three alternative modes of transport, road, rail, and direct ferry, already existed.

The road route was quite circuitous; the rail route involved transshipment between broad gauge and meter gauge; a ferry or the LCT (loading craft terminal) involved delays, or extra handlings and the nonavailability of the ferry except at fixed hours and that too during day light hours.

Project proposal analysis involved estimation of financial inflows and outflows.

Analysis of the expected social costs–benefits involved the assessment of the following:

- Total annual movement of traffic and cargo—South to North and North to South—both goods and traffic. Commodity-wise traffic was forecast till the 11th year after the opening of the bridge and beyond that benefits were assumed to be constant.
- Projection of unsatisfied demand, that is, increase in the movement of goods and service.
- Estimation of benefits and costs, that is, inflows and outflows for the expected traffic and also for projected unsatisfied demand.
- Estimation of social benefits and costs.
- Social benefits were revenues in terms of
  - Savings in costs resulting from reduction in vehicle operating costs and saving of fuel and road maintenance costs, or

- ○ Increase in revenue arising from movement of goods and services like vegetables or milk which earlier were not transported due to their perishable nature.
- Social costs arose from increase in unemployment or increase in the level of pollution. For example, bridge constructed reduced the number of ferry plying both ways and that lead to unemployment of certain persons.
- Thus IRR on investment was worked out, computing benefits in terms of quantifiable saving in costs to economy by using the proposed bridge.
- IRR was calculated for the construction of the bridge at two different locations. Further, for each location, there were four alternatives, namely, for moderate and pessimistic traffic with "no cost overrun" and 10% "cost overrun," respectively.
- In addition, a sensitivity analysis was also carried out taking the existence of another bridge.

Case Studies

Case Study: Tata and AirAsia Airways Project

Tata Group planned to join AirAsia Bhd., Asia's largest low-fare carrier and a local investor to enter the aviation market. It was 13 years after the Tata's bid to buy 40 percent stake in Air India in partnership with Singapore Airlines Ltd which collapsed in the face of political and corporate intrigue; Air India originally was founded by Tata Group as Tata Airlines in the 1930s which was nationalized in 1953.

AirAsia is Asia's largest low-fare carrier with 118 planes and more than 350 on order. Tony Fernandes, founder and group chief executive of AirAsia, an Indian extraction on his father side, evaluated developments in India over the last few years and was of the view that "the current environment is perfect to introduce AirAsia's low fares, which stimulate travel and grow the market." Further, AirAsia believed that, "India aviation has enormous long-term growth potential and is expected to produce tremendous upside for first movers." AirAsia planned to replicate its success in Malaysia, Thailand, and Indonesia and focused on big Asian markets such as India through joint ventures (JVs).

The proposed airlines would be a JV between three parties, namely, Malaysia-based AirAsia, Tata Sons, and Telestra Tradeplace Pvt Ltd. AirAsia would hold 49 percent share, Tata Sons would have 30 percent, and the remaining 21 percent by the third partner. The initial investment in the project is estimated to be $30 to $60 million (Rs. 185–330 crores).

The airline would be managed by AirAsia, and Tata Sons would not have any operating role in the proposed venture. It would be proper to mention that Tata Group owned nearly 6 percent stake in SpiceJet Ltd, India's second largest low-fare carrier and it was just a financial investment.

Telestra Tradeplace Pvt Ltd headed by Arun Bhatia was associated with AirAsia founder Tony Fernandes at the football club of which Fernandes was the club chairman.

Tata Sons was entering into the proposed venture given the reputed business model of AirAsia and that AirAsia could be a relevant and successful service provider in the domestic market. The domestic market was expected to draw benefits which included (a) AirAsia's reputed service, which would further grow aviation as a mode of transport in what was a relatively underserved market, and (b) employment generation.

Telestra Tradeplace, the third partner, had a presence in aerospace with a group company called Hindustan Aerosystems Pvt Ltd, which manufactures and supplies precision components for the industry. Arun Bhatia's son Amit Bhatia served on the board of directors at Queens Park Rangers Football Club in the United Kingdom alongside Fernandes, who was the majority owner of the club.

AirAsia had submitted an application to the Foreign Investment Promotion Board (FIPB) seeking approval to invest 49 percent in the venture. Thereafter, an application would be made by the proposed JV company to the Indian aviation regulators for the air operations permit.

As such, the AirAsia application was the first seeking approval to form a new airline after the liberalization of India's overseas investment rules in aviation in September 2012 under which overseas airlines were allowed to pick up a stake up to 49 percent in domestic carriers. As per that liberalization policy, United Arab Emirates carrier Etihad Airways PISC was planning to buy a 24 percent stake in Jet Airways (India) Ltd.

The proposed JV planned to operate from Chennai, Tamil Nadu, and would provide domestic tier II/tier III city connectivity to Indian travelers. The focus will be on smaller cities that could handle Airbus SAS A320 operations and not to fly to high-cost airports. The single-plane model would allow the company to keep the costs low. The company won't consider using smaller 70-seater planes and planned to start with three—four planes and scale up in the future. The company was hiring an all-Indian senior management and would start with about 300 employees. Currently, AirAsia, through its operations based in Thailand and Malaysia, already connects Chennai, Bengaluru, Tiruchirappalli, Kochi, and Kolkata to ASEAN; ASEAN stands for the Association of Southeast Asian Nations. AirAsia already operated 45 flights weekly from India to Kuala Lumpur.

Such associations with foreign airlines were at a time when India's airline industry was laden with heavy debt and years of accumulated losses, rising costs, and intense competition. It was viewed that "India with its low flyer base, regulatory challenges and high cost structure, cannot afford more than four strong national airlines" and consolidation was expected like that happening in the United States and the European Union.

It was also viewed that the new venture would develop new markets between India and Southeast Asia. To quote, Craige Jenks, president of Airline/Aircraft Projects Inc., a leading New York-based air transport consulting and advisory services firm, "Up to now, Indian private airlines have followed Air India's footsteps. They see goldmines in Dubai or Singapore, and their strategy is then to get into that already existing gold mine. The mind-set of AirAsia has been 100 percent opposite, and to develop a market where none previously existed. So I don't think it is primarily an ultra-low-cost attack on what is already there, I think it is probably about creating new markets."

Though the entry of AirAsia would change the landscape of competition in India, it was not going to be smooth for AirAsia as it enjoyed significant infrastructure advantage, including separate low-cost terminals. Indian market was different as it was facing huge infrastructure shortage and Indian conditions will not be as friendly as those in Malaysia. Further, AirAsia won't be able to rely just on secondary Indian airports as the airline may not get sufficient passenger traffic.

In this regard, said Prof. Nawal Taneja, professor emeritus at the department of aviation at Ohio State University, "'One brand, multiple production units is the new trend.' It started with Lan Airlines in Latin America and then spread to Asia with Air Asia and in Australia with Jetstar. It is the way of the future." (*Source:* P.R. Sanjai, *Mint* February 21, 2013)

Case Study: State Electricity Board Expansion Proposal Project

State Electricity Board, taking advantage of the government economic reforms and the liberalization measures announced, is planning to expand by setting up a gas-based power-generating unit.

The management of SEB has worked out a proposal to expand by adding a gas-based power-generating plant. Building for expansion would cost Rs. 600 lakhs; plant costing Rs. 1,200 lakhs is to be purchased from Bangalore requiring transportation, insurance, and installation expenses of Rs. 50 lakhs each. Working capital requirements are estimated at Rs. 200 lakhs. It is estimated that the pretests and trial run would cost another Rs.500 lakhs; the trial run would yield an output valued at Rs. 150 lakhs.

The unit is likely to operate at 50% in the first 2 years and at 70% thereafter for the remaining life of 3 years. The unit would be operational in the first year and there would be no gestation period. Thus the unit is estimated to have a life of 5 years at the expiry of which it would realize Rs. 800 lakhs.

The plant has an installed capacity to generate 10 lakh units a day which could be sold at an administered price of Rs. 2.00 per unit (assume 300 working days a year).

Estimates for operating cost for the 5 years are as under:

		Years		(Rs. Lakhs)	
	1	2	3	4	5
Material	600	600	850	850	850
Manpower	900	900	1,450	1,450	1,450
Others	500	500	900	900	900
Depreciation	300	300	300	300	300
Interest	100	100	100	100	100
Total	2,400	2,400	3,600	3,600	3,600

Assignment:

A: Financial Analysis

- Estimate project cost
- Estimate annual operating costs
- Estimate annual operating revenue
- Estimate annual inflows and outflows
- Suggest possible alternative sources of funds
- Evaluate the project and advise on the economic viability of the project

B: Social Cost–Benefit Analysis

- For construction of building, the company is getting $6,000 to import cement and steel at control rate. The open market price is 25 percent higher.
- The administered price per unit of electricity is Rs. 2 while the market price is Rs. 3 per unit.
- The manpower cost at the minimum wage rate is 160 percent of international price.

Sustainability of the Project Over Its Lifetime

Given the future orientation of any project, it would be logical to consider the full lifetime of any project, from its conception to its disposal. It can be argued that when considering sustainability in project management the total life of the project and not just the life-cycle of the project is relevant; for example, if we take a city metro rail project, then we should consider not just the cumulative costs of activities/tasks that form part of launching this project but also the periodic costs of rebuilding/repairing the worn out parts of this asset, namely, stations and escalators. Most developed nations, not having considered this all important dimension before setting up large infrastructure projects in the mid-early twentieth century, are now facing the challenge, funds crunch for replacing/renovating/upgrading their aged infrastructure.

Annexure I: Present Value Table of Rs. 1

$$PVIF_{i,n} = 1/(1+i)^n = 1/FVIF_{i,n}$$

	1%	2%	3%	4%	5%	6%	7%	8%	9%	10%	11%	12%	13%	14%	15%	16%	17%	18%	19%	20%
1	0.99	0.98	0.971	0.962	0.952	0.943	0.935	0.926	0.917	0.909	0.901	0.893	0.885	0.877	0.87	0.862	0.855	0.847	0.84	0.833
2	0.98	0.961	0.943	0.925	0.907	0.89	0.873	0.857	0.842	0.826	0.812	0.797	0.783	0.769	0.756	0.743	0.731	0.718	0.706	0.694
3	0.971	0.942	0.915	0.889	0.864	0.84	0.816	0.794	0.772	0.751	0.731	0.712	0.693	0.675	0.658	0.641	0.624	0.609	0.593	0.579
4	0.961	0.924	0.888	0.855	0.823	0.792	0.763	0.735	0.708	0.683	0.659	0.636	0.613	0.592	0.572	0.552	0.534	0.516	0.499	0.482
5	0.951	0.906	0.863	0.822	0.784	0.747	0.713	0.681	0.65	0.621	0.593	0.567	0.543	0.519	0.497	0.476	0.456	0.437	0.419	0.402
6	0.942	0.888	0.837	0.79	0.746	0.705	0.666	0.63	0.596	0.564	0.535	0.507	0.48	0.456	0.432	0.41	0.39	0.37	0.352	0.335
7	0.933	0.871	0.813	0.76	0.711	0.665	0.623	0.583	0.547	0.513	0.482	0.452	0.425	0.4	0.376	0.354	0.333	0.314	0.296	0.279
8	0.923	0.853	0.789	0.731	0.677	0.627	0.582	0.54	0.502	0.467	0.434	0.404	0.376	0.351	0.327	0.305	0.285	0.266	0.249	0.233
9	0.914	0.837	0.766	0.703	0.645	0.592	0.544	0.5	0.46	0.424	0.391	0.361	0.333	0.308	0.294	0.283	0.243	0.225	0.209	0.194
10	0.905	0.82	0.744	0.676	0.614	0.558	0.508	0.463	0.422	0.386	0.352	0.322	0.295	0.27	0.247	0.227	0.206	0.191	0.176	0.162
11	0.896	0.804	0.722	0.65	0.585	0.527	0.475	0.429	0.388	0.35	0.317	0.287	0.261	0.237	0.215	0.195	0.178	0.162	0.148	0.136
12	0.887	0.788	0.701	0.625	0.557	0.497	0.444	0.397	0.356	0.319	0.286	0.257	0.231	0.208	0.187	0.168	0.152	0.137	0.124	0.112
13	0.879	0.773	0.681	0.601	0.53	0.469	0.415	0.368	0.326	0.29	0.258	0.229	0.204	0.182	0.163	0.145	0.13	0.116	0.104	0.093
14	0.87	0.758	0.661	0.577	0.506	0.442	0.388	0.34	0.299	0.263	0.232	0.205	0.181	0.16	0.141	0.125	0.111	0.099	0.088	0.078
15	0.861	0.743	0.642	0.555	0.481	0.417	0.362	0.315	0.275	0.239	0.209	0.183	0.16	0.14	0.123	0.108	0.095	0.084	0.074	0.065
16	0.853	0.728	0.623	0.534	0.458	0.394	0.339	0.292	0.252	0.218	0.188	0.163	0.141	0.123	0.107	0.093	0.081	0.071	0.062	0.054
17	0.844	0.714	0.605	0.513	0.436	0.371	0.317	0.27	0.231	0.198	0.17	0.146	0.125	0.108	0.093	0.08	0.069	0.06	0.052	0.045
18	0.836	0.7	0.587	0.494	0.416	0.35	0.296	0.25	0.212	0.18	0.153	0.13	0.111	0.095	0.081	0.069	0.059	0.051	0.044	0.038
19	0.828	0.686	0.57	0.475	0.396	0.331	0.277	0.232	0.194	0.164	0.138	0.116	0.098	0.083	0.07	0.06	0.051	0.043	0.037	0.031

20	0.026	0.031	0.037	0.043	0.051	0.061	0.073	0.087	0.104	0.124	0.149	0.178	0.215	0.258	0.312	0.377	0.456	0.554	0.673	0.82
21	0.022	0.026	0.031	0.037	0.044	0.053	0.064	0.077	0.093	0.112	0.135	0.164	0.199	0.242	0.294	0.359	0.439	0.538	0.66	0.811
22	0.018	0.022	0.026	0.032	0.038	0.046	0.056	0.068	0.083	0.101	0.123	0.15	0.184	0.226	0.278	0.342	0.422	0.522	0.647	0.803
23	0.015	0.018	0.022	0.027	0.033	0.04	0.049	0.06	0.074	0.091	0.112	0.138	0.17	0.211	0.262	0.326	0.406	0.507	0.634	0.795
24	0.013	0.015	0.019	0.023	0.028	0.035	0.043	0.053	0.066	0.082	0.102	0.126	0.158	0.197	0.247	0.31	0.39	0.492	0.622	0.788
25	0.01	0.013	0.016	0.02	0.024	0.03	0.038	0.047	0.059	0.074	0.092	0.116	0.146	0.184	0.233	0.296	0.375	0.478	0.61	0.78
26	0.009	0.011	0.014	0.017	0.021	0.026	0.033	0.042	0.053	0.066	0.084	0.106	0.135	0.172	0.22	0.281	0.361	0.464	0.598	0.772
27	0.007	0.009	0.011	0.014	0.018	0.023	0.029	0.037	0.047	0.06	0.076	0.098	0.125	0.161	0.207	0.268	0.347	0.45	0.586	0.764
28	0.006	0.008	0.01	0.012	0.016	0.02	0.026	0.033	0.042	0.054	0.069	0.09	0.116	0.15	0.196	0.255	0.333	0.437	0.574	0.757
29	0.005	0.006	0.008	0.011	0.014	0.017	0.022	0.029	0.037	0.048	0.063	0.082	0.107	0.141	0.185	0.243	0.321	0.424	0.583	0.749
30	0.004	0.005	0.007	0.009	0.012	0.015	0.02	0.026	0.033	0.044	0.057	0.075	0.099	0.131	0.174	0.231	0.308	0.412	0.552	0.742
31	0.004	0.005	0.006	0.008	0.01	0.013	0.017	0.023	0.03	0.039	0.052	0.069	0.092	0.123	0.164	0.22	0.296	0.4	0.541	0.735
32	0.003	0.004	0.005	0.007	0.009	0.011	0.015	0.02	0.027	0.035	0.047	0.063	0.085	0.115	0.155	0.21	0.285	0.388	0.531	0.727
33	0.002	0.003	0.004	0.006	0.007	0.01	0.013	0.018	0.024	0.032	0.043	0.058	0.079	0.107	0.146	0.2	0.274	0.377	0.52	0.72
34	0.002	0.003	0.004	0.005	0.006	0.009	0.012	0.016	0.021	0.029	0.039	0.053	0.073	0.1	0.138	0.19	0.264	0.366	0.51	0.713
35	0.002	0.002	0.003	0.004	0.006	0.008	0.01	0.014	0.019	0.026	0.036	0.049	0.068	0.094	0.13	0.181	0.253	0.355	0.5	0.706
36	0.002	0.002	0.003	0.004	0.005	0.007	0.009	0.012	0.017	0.023	0.032	0.045	0.063	0.088	0.123	0.173	0.244	0.345	0.49	0.699
37	0.001	0.002	0.002	0.003	0.004	0.006	0.008	0.011	0.015	0.021	0.029	0.041	0.058	0.082	0.116	0.164	0.234	0.335	0.481	0.692
38	0.001	0.002	0.002	0.003	0.004	0.005	0.007	0.01	0.013	0.019	0.027	0.038	0.054	0.076	0.109	0.157	0.225	0.325	0.471	0.685
39	0.001	0.001	0.002	0.002	0.003	0.004	0.006	0.009	0.012	0.017	0.024	0.035	0.05	0.071	0.103	0.149	0.217	0.316	0.462	0.678
40	0.001	0.001	0.001	0.002	0.003	0.004	0.005	0.006	0.011	0.015	0.022	0.032	0.046	0.067	0.097	0.142	0.206	0.307	0.453	0.672

Annexure II: Future Value of Rs. 1

$$FVIF_{i,n} = (1 + i)^n$$

	1%	2%	3%	4%	5%	6%	7%	8%	9%	10%	11%	12%	13%	14%	15%	16%	17%	18%	19%	20%
1	1.01	1.02	1.03	1.04	1.05	1.06	1.07	1.08	1.09	1.1	1.11	1.12	1.13	1.14	1.15	1.16	1.17	1.18	1.19	1.2
2	1.02	1.04	1.061	1.082	1.103	1.124	1.145	1.166	1.188	1.21	1.232	1.254	1.277	1.3	1.323	1.346	1.369	1.392	1.416	1.44
3	1.03	1.061	1.093	1.125	1.158	1.191	1.225	1.26	1.295	1.331	1.368	1.405	1.443	1.482	1.521	1.561	1.602	1.643	1.685	1.728
4	1.041	1.082	1.126	1.17	1.216	1.262	1.311	1.36	1.412	1.464	1.518	1.574	1.63	1.689	1.749	1.811	1.874	1.939	2.005	2.074
5	1.051	1.104	1.159	1.217	1.276	1.338	1.403	1.469	1.539	1.611	1.685	1.762	1.842	1.925	2.011	2.1	2.192	2.288	2.386	2.488
6	1.062	1.126	1.194	1.265	1.34	1.419	1.501	1.587	1.677	1.772	1.87	1.974	2.082	2.195	2.313	2.436	2.565	2.7	2.84	2.986
7	1.072	1.149	1.23	1.316	1.407	1.504	1.606	1.714	1.828	1.949	2.076	2.211	2.353	2.502	2.66	2.826	3.001	3.185	3.379	3.583
8	1.083	1.172	1.267	1.369	1.477	1.594	1.718	1.851	1.993	2.144	2.305	2.476	2.658	2.853	3.059	3.278	3.511	3.759	4.021	4.3
9	1.094	1.195	1.305	1.423	1.551	1.689	1.838	1.999	2.172	2.358	2.558	2.773	3.004	3.252	3.518	3.803	4.108	4.435	4.785	5.16
10	1.105	1.218	1.344	1.48	1.629	1.791	1.967	2.159	2.367	2.594	2.839	3.106	3.395	3.707	4.046	4.411	4.807	5.234	5.695	6.192
11	1.116	1.243	1.384	1.539	1.71	1.898	2.105	2.332	2.58	2.853	3.152	3.479	3.836	4.226	4.652	5.117	5.624	6.176	6.777	7.43
12	1.127	1.268	1.426	1.601	1.796	2.012	2.252	2.518	2.813	3.138	3.498	3.896	4.335	4.818	5.35	5.936	6.58	7.288	8.064	8.916
13	1.138	1.294	1.469	1.665	1.886	2.133	2.41	2.72	3.066	3.452	3.883	4.363	4.898	5.492	6.153	6.886	7.699	8.599	9.596	10.669
14	1.149	1.319	1.513	1.732	1.98	2.261	2.579	2.937	3.342	3.797	4.31	4.887	5.535	6.261	7.076	7.988	9.007	10.147	11.42	12.839
15	1.161	1.346	1.558	1.801	2.079	2.397	2.759	3.172	3.642	4.177	4.785	5.474	6.254	7.138	8.137	9.266	10.539	11.974	13.59	15.407
16	1.173	1.373	1.605	1.873	2.183	2.54	2.952	3.426	3.97	4.595	5.311	6.13	7.067	8.137	9.358	10.748	12.33	14.129	16.172	18.488
17	1.184	1.4	1.653	1.948	2.292	2.693	3.159	3.7	4.328	5.054	5.895	6.866	7.986	9.276	10.761	12.468	14.426	16.672	19.244	22.186
18	1.196	1.428	1.702	2.026	2.407	2.854	3.38	3.996	4.717	5.56	6.544	7.69	9.024	10.575	12.375	14.463	16.879	19.673	22.901	26.623
19	1.208	1.457	1.754	2.107	2.527	3.026	3.617	4.316	5.142	6.116	7.263	8.613	10.197	12.056	14.232	16.777	19.748	23.214	27.252	31.948
20	1.22	1.486	1.806	2.191	2.653	3.207	3.87	4.661	5.604	6.727	8.062	9.646	11.523	13.743	16.367	19.461	23.106	27.393	32.429	38.338
21	1.232	1.516	1.86	2.279	2.786	3.4	4.141	5.034	6.109	7.4	8.949	10.804	13.021	15.668	18.822	22.574	27.034	32.324	38.591	46.005
22	1.245	1.546	1.916	2.37	2.925	3.604	4.43	5.437	6.659	8.14	9.934	12.1	14.714	17.861	21.645	26.186	31.629	38.142	45.923	55.206

23	1.257	1.577	1.974	2.465	3.072	3.82	4.741	5.871	7.258	8.954	11.026	13.552	16.627	20.362	24.891	30.376	37.006	45.008	54.649	66.247
24	1.27	1.608	2.033	2.563	3.225	4.049	5.072	6.341	7.911	9.85	12.239	15.179	18.788	23.212	28.625	35.236	43.297	53.109	65.032	79.497
25	1.282	1.641	2.094	2.666	3.386	4.292	5.427	6.848	8.623	10.835	13.585	17	21.231	26.462	32.919	40.874	50.658	62.669	77.388	95.396
26	1.295	1.673	2.157	2.772	3.556	4.549	5.807	7.396	9.399	11.918	15.08	19.04	23.991	30.167	37.857	47.414	59.27	73.949	92.092	114.475
27	1.308	1.707	2.221	2.883	3.733	4.822	6.214	7.988	10.245	13.11	16.739	21.325	27.109	34.39	43.535	55	69.345	87.26	109.589	137.371
28	1.321	1.741	2.288	2.999	3.92	5.112	6.649	8.627	11.167	14.421	18.58	23.884	30.633	39.204	50.066	63.8	81.134	102.967	130.411	164.845
29	1.335	1.776	2.357	3.119	4.116	5.418	7.114	9.317	12.172	15.863	20.624	26.75	34.616	44.693	57.575	74.009	94.927	121.501	155.189	197.814
30	1.348	1.811	2.427	3.243	4.322	5.743	7.612	10.063	13.268	17.449	22.892	29.96	39.116	50.95	66.212	85.85	111.065	143.371	184.675	237.376
31	1.361	1.848	2.5	3.373	4.538	6.088	8.145	10.868	14.462	19.194	25.41	33.555	44.201	58.083	76.144	99.586	129.946	169.177	219.764	284.852
32	1.375	1.885	2.575	3.508	4.765	6.453	8.715	11.737	15.763	21.114	28.206	37.582	49.947	66.215	87.565	115.52	152.036	199.629	261.519	341.822
33	1.389	1.922	2.652	3.648	5.003	6.841	9.325	12.676	17.182	23.225	31.308	42.092	56.44	75.485	100.7	134.003	177.883	235.563	311.207	410.186
34	1.403	1.961	2.732	3.794	5.253	7.251	9.978	13.69	18.728	25.548	34.752	47.143	63.777	86.053	115.805	155.443	208.123	277.964	370.337	492.224
35	1.417	2	2.814	3.946	5.516	7.686	10.677	14.785	20.414	28.102	38.575	52.8	72.069	98.1	133.176	180.314	243.503	327.997	440.701	590.668
36	1.431	2.04	2.898	4.104	5.792	8.147	11.424	15.968	22.251	30.913	42.818	59.136	81.437	111.834	153.152	209.164	284.899	387.037	524.434	708.802
37	1.445	2.081	2.985	4.268	6.081	8.636	12.224	17.246	24.254	34.004	47.528	66.232	92.024	127.491	176.125	242.631	333.332	456.703	624.076	850.562
38	1.46	2.122	3.075	4.439	6.385	9.154	13.079	18.625	26.437	37.404	52.756	74.18	103.987	145.34	202.543	281.452	389.998	538.91	742.651	1,020.675
39	1.474	2.165	3.167	4.616	6.705	9.704	13.995	20.115	28.816	41.145	58.559	83.081	117.506	165.687	232.925	326.484	456.298	635.914	883.754	1,224.81
40	1.489	2.208	3.262	4.801	7.04	10.286	14.947	21.725	31.409	45.259	65.001	93.051	132.782	188.884	267.864	378.721	533.869	750.378	1,051.668	1,469.772

Index

OTHER TITLES IN OUR PORTFOLIO AND PROJECT MANAGEMENT COLLECTION

Timothy J. Kloppenborg, *Editor*

- *Attributes of Project-Friendly Enterprises* by Vittal S. Anantatmula and Parviz F. Rad
- *Stakeholder-led Project Management: Changing the Way We Manage Projects* by Louise Worsley
- *KNOWledge SUCCESSion: Sustained Performance and Capability Growth Through Strategic Knowledge Projects* by Arthur Shelley
- *Improving Executive Sponsorship of Projects: A Holistic Approach* by Dawne Chandler and *Payson Hall*
- *Innovative Business Projects: Breaking Complexities, Building Performance, Volume I; Fundamentals and Project Environment* by Rajagopal
- *Innovative Business Projects: Breaking Complexities, Building Performance, Volume II; Financials, New Insights, and Project Sustainability* by Rajagopal
- *Co-Create: Harnessing the Human Element in Project Management* by Steve Martin

Announcing the Business Expert Press Digital Library

Concise e-books business students need for classroom and research

This book can also be purchased in an e-book collection by your library as

- a one-time purchase,
- that is owned forever,
- allows for simultaneous readers,
- has no restrictions on printing, and
- can be downloaded as PDFs from within the library community.

Our digital library collections are a great solution to beat the rising cost of textbooks. E-books can be loaded into their course management systems or onto students' e-book readers.
The **Business Expert Press** digital libraries are very affordable, with no obligation to buy in future years. For more information, please visit **www.businessexpertpress.com/librarians**. To set up a trial in the United States, please email **sales@businessexpertpress.com**.

www.ingramcontent.com/pod-product-compliance
Lightning Source LLC
Chambersburg PA
CBHW071505200326
41519CB00019B/5876

9 7 8 1 6 0 6 4 9 6 6 8 8